Effective Customer Care

THE SUNDAY TIMES

Effective Customer Care

Pat Wellington

LONDON PHILADELPHIA NEW DELHI

For my inspirational colleague Patrick Forsyth

Publisher's note

First published in Great Britain and the United States in 2010 by Kogan Page Limited

120 Pentonville Road
London N1 9JN
United Kingdom
www.koganpage.com

525 South 4th Street, #241
Philadelphia PA 19147
USA

4737/23 Ansari Road
Daryaganj
New Delhi 110002
India

© Pat Wellington, 2010

ISBN 978 0 7494 5997 0
E-ISBN 978 0 7494 5998 7

British Library Cataloguing-in-Publication Data

A CIP record for this book is available from the British Library.

Library of Congress Cataloging-in-Publication Data

Wellington, Patricia.
    Effective customer care / Pat Wellington.
        p. cm.
    ISBN 978-0-7494-5997-0 -- ISBN 978-0-7494-5998-7 (ebk) 1. Customer relations. 2. Customer services. 3. Customer relations--Case studies. 4. Customer services--Case studies. I. Title.
    HF5415.5.W449 2010
    658.8'12--dc22
                                    2009050536

Typeset by Saxon Graphics Ltd, Derby
Printed and bound in India by Replika Press Pvt Ltd

Contents

About the author

Pat Wellington is a popular international speaker and busy consultant. Her specialisms are customer care and business development, leadership, the management of change, and team building. Her particular expertise is to ensure that Kaizen (continuous improvement) is incorporated into her programmes. This not only enriches people's lives at all levels within an organisation, but also brings very tangible results in terms of increased productivity and profitability.

Pat has many years of practical experience as well as a thorough theoretical grounding. She knows from first-hand experience the issues that those in a customer contact role have to tackle. At the start of her business career she spent several years working in customer contact and sales management in the retail sector, servicing leading department stores including Harvey Nichols, Liberty, the Bentalls Group and House of Fraser. She then moved into the IT sector in a customer management role working with clients from mainframe and software organisations including IBM and Sterling Software.

Fifteen years ago she moved into consultancy, initially joining Marketing Improvements where she delivered customer care and business development training both on a public-course and in-house basis. She then moved to City University, joining the Management Development Centre where she devised key account management strategies for, among others, the Bank of England and Abbey National Treasury. In 2000 she headed up the Management Development Unit of London Metropolitan University, the largest educational establishment in the UK capital, and in 2006 became Director of Europe Japan Management, a consultancy group specialising in the best of East and West management practices.

The consultancy and training assignments she has undertaken have been numerous and diverse and in most industry sectors including healthcare, manufacturing, IT and the service sector, plus a variety of government bodies. She is an enthusiastic and motivational facilitator and has helped managers and front-line professionals gain skills and knowledge, and importantly become more productive on returning to their workplace. A few comments from delegates that have attended her programmes:

a very enriching workshop...
lively and practical...
full of ideas that I can use when I get back to work...

In the UK she has worked for blue-chip organisations such as Canon and Coates Viyella, private hospital chains such as the Nuffield and the St Martin's hospital groups; in the government sector she has project-managed MBA programmes.

In mainland Europe she has worked with three United Nations agencies in Rome and with the UNHCR in Geneva. Also within Europe she has undertaken a major research assignment for Coca-Cola, and aided at a strategic level within a high-tech organisation in Switzerland. In the Gulf, Pat has delivered sessions and key note presentations for petrochemical organisations, the government of Dubai and Zamil Steel.

In south-east Asia she regularly delivers seminars for the Institute of Management in Singapore, and has been a guest speaker at conferences in Kuala Lumpur and Indonesia. She has undertaken in-house projects in customer care for the regional Civil Aviation Authority, and assisted with the privatisation of a leading water authority in Malaysia.

Pat has written many articles and books including *Kaizen Strategies for Customer Care* (FT/Prentice Hall), and contributed to *Kaizen Strategies for Improving Team Performance*. Her most recent publication is *Effective Team Leadership for Engineers* (IET).

If you would like to share any of your customer care experiences with Pat, she would welcome hearing from you. Contact her at pat@pwellington.plus.com.

About this book

For many years we have been told that the customer is king; but how often do you as a customer actually feel as if you are being treated as a king (or queen, for that matter)?!

In stores, assistants seem invisible or too busy on the telephone. Organisations set up obstacle courses of button-pushing options; and too often when you do make contact, people are uninformed or unhelpful (and sometimes downright rude). When they should be making doing business with them a pleasure, they turn you off and ensure you will never want to deal with them again. 'How can I help you?' has come to carry all the sincerity of an old chestnut like 'The cheque is in the post.'

Something is not quite working as it should – at least not from the customer's perspective. But it does not have to be like this in your organisation.

This book is for any manager who cares about customer care, wants to offer excellent customer service and also wants to create a productive and happy working environment for both themself and their team.

What are organisations doing to improve the service they offer to customers?

Back in the distant past, working in a customer service department was a pretty thankless task. It might well have been concerned mostly with complaints and problem resolution, its status was low, unlike marketing or sales, and staff often saw their time there only as a stepping stone to better things.

Over the last two decades, however, there has been a shift in thinking within organisations. There has been a realisation that many products and services have become largely indistinguishable, and the one way that a company can differentiate itself, thrive and be profitable is by the quality of service it can offer to customers.

Not only has this enhanced the profile of the customer service department, but changes have been made throughout organisations to improve the service offered to customers. Total quality management initiatives have been undertaken, company-wide training programmes introduced and technological advances made to aid the ease of access to customer data. Despite this, customers still find something, well, let's just say, less than they want.

Numerous books on customer care have been written, usually with two target audiences in mind: front-line staff and senior management. For front-line staff, books have focused on how to answer the phone, smile and nurture the customer. For senior management, the message has focused on strategic management issues – the big picture – and how to make the whole company more customer focused and competitive.

I have worked for many years delivering customer care training programmes at every level in organisations. In researching materials for these programmes I came to realise that relatively little had been written on customer service for middle managers – the very people that are ultimately accountable for the front-line staff delivering service. These front-line staff represent the public image of the organisation. How they deal with customers literally dictates whether a customer will buy a product or service and become or continue to be a loyal customer or not. However, they are only as good as the direction and support they receive from their managers, and the service chain within their organisation. If they don't get the back-up they require, delivering an appropriate level of service is impossible.

So it is up to middle managers and team leaders to ensure that they create the environment in which members of their team can flourish. This emphasis on environment is crucial. It means getting staff to be more than purely task focused. There might be great systems, procedures and technology in place, but none of these on their own ensure effective customer service. Only people can do this. Hence this book.

It offers robust information on the whole customer care process, and how to build long-term partnerships both with customers and your suppliers. In addition, a chapter is dedicated to helping you create a productive, focused team spirit, which encourages everyone to push the boundaries, be creative and willing to go the extra mile, and offer a value-added service to customers.

As a manager you also need to be able to get cooperation, action and an agreed level of service from the other teams or departments who relate to your activity. This can often be easier said than done! So the book also has a chapter dedicated to this thorny issue.

The book is arranged accessibly so that busy managers can dip into different sections as and when required. You will find key information about particular topics, brought to life by case examples, checklists and, where appropriate, brief exercises to show you in more detail how things work and what is meant by a particular phrase or expression.

Ultimately the purpose of this book is to give you the tools and techniques required to be an effective manager and able to create a positively motivated and customer-focused team, whose members will go the extra mile to satisfy the customer. This will result in a reduction of complaints and improved customer retention and bottom-line results, all of which ultimately mean more job security for you and your team in these challenging economic times.

Surely these are worthwhile aims for anyone. Remember that good customer service is not an option; in today's dynamic markets it is a must if you are to outperform competition.

Pat Wellington
Europe Japan Management
E-mail: pat@pwellington.plus.com
Tel: + 44 (0)774 0022735

Introduction: putting customer care in context

> There is only one boss. The customer. And he or she can fire everybody in the company from the chairman down, simply by spending their money somewhere else.
>
> *(Sam Walton, founder of Wal-Mart)*

Customer care: two simple words but what do they mean? We are all customers for something. Sometimes we want a prompt no-nonsense form of service. Sometimes we need lengthy advice. But often the service we receive is poor or nonexistent. And occasionally we are delighted by what happens when we buy a particular product or service, or note how well we are taken care of by an individual in a company and decide, in the back of our mind, to use that supplier in the future. We are a happy customer.

Being a happy customer means that we are more likely to be loyal. Being loyal means that we may buy more from the same organisation, even though that may sometimes mean paying a bit extra. Why? Because we don't want to go to another supplier and take the risk of not being satisfied again.

This all may seem quite straightforward, but just think about it. In reality how often are you really a satisfied customer?

Deliveries can turn up late. You can be put on hold on a telephone helpline service with the inevitable 'Greensleeves' being played for 20 interminable minutes while you wait to get through to a real person. Or you are faced with a surly individual across a counter who looks as if they have been watching the W C Fields film in which he says, 'Start the day with a smile and get it over with' – and they have not even been moved to adopt that philosophy.

As a customer in these circumstances you will often go elsewhere for the product or service, and usually won't let the company that has served you poorly know why you have left. An average of 65 per cent of all potential business is lost by suppliers due to their staff's apparent lack of interest, lack of attention to customers' needs and failure to meet customers' expectations.

The reality is as follows. If someone is unhappy with the service they receive from you they typically tell 10 others. With the internet, one click means that this information can now be spread to a whole community in no time at all. Think about this in the context of the substantial spend involved in acquiring new customers through advertising, telemarketing, TV campaigns and the setting up of a new account in the sales system, in customer service and in credit control. All this adds cost – totally unnecessarily.

> According to the *Harvard Business Review*, if you can reduce customer defections by just 5 per cent you can increase profitability by between 25 and 85 per cent!

In many ways good customer care costs no more than bad – doing it well is a real opportunity to boost profitability.

One thing is for sure. There's a customer revolution taking place. More and more products and services are becoming alike. There's so much choice: choice of supplier, choice of channel, choice of products and choice of services.

The real question to ask is, 'How do your products or services stand out from the crowd?' Differentiation is the order of the day.

Good customer service is not an option, it's a must. Sometimes it can be difficult – and so can customers – but as the old saying has it, this is no worse than no customers.

So how do you move from a simple service provider to a 'service partner' position? In other words, how do you become a first-choice supplier with your customers? How do you build brand loyalty and maximise profitability? How can your organisation add real value to the way your customer service works? How can you maximise your customers' experience so they return not just once but time after time, and encourage other organisations or individuals to do the same?

This is what this book is about.

It examines the means, the resources and, importantly, the attitudes needed to create a more customer-focused organisation. It will explain the 'how' of delivering clearly defined customer-care behaviours, help you with problem solving and getting the cooperation you need from others. It will also explain why excellence in customer care is essential to your organisation's business growth and survival.

The quality of service that your customers experience is ultimately influenced by one thing – your people. Your front-line staff bear prime responsibility for taking care of your customers, but everybody in the service chain has an impact one way or another, and the quality of this stems from their attitude and level of enthusiasm for their job. It is your role and ultimate responsibility as a manager to make sure the service those in your team offer to the customer not only works just adequately, or by the skin of its teeth, but is outstanding. Anything less is missing a trick.

1

The fundamentals of customer care

Businesses are not paid to reform customers. They are paid to satisfy customers.

(Peter Drucker)

Introduction

Organisations use a variety of methods to make sure that their customers and suppliers actually know they exist.

Starting from the big picture they commission advertising campaigns, undertake corporate sponsorship of events or enter their company for an industry award. To let everyone know exactly what they do, brochures are produced, websites created, directory entries made, newsletters circulated to their database, articles are written by members of staff and published in customer or supplier trade press. To show they are one step ahead of the competition, key members of staff make presentations at conferences or industry-specific round-table events. There is corporate hospitality with a view to attracting new customers, and the business development team are out around the country or travelling the world generating new business.

All of this activity to create business growth and a feel-good factor about an organisation that can be destroyed in a moment by poor customer care.

Customer service is not a department; it is an attitude. The concept of 'service' and 'care' can be difficult to describe in tangible terms. And yet in every service encounter there are tangibles – before, during and after the exchange between both parties – which affect how customers judge the quality of service that is being provided.

So – the sixty-four thousand dollar question – what is it that goes through a customer's mind, sometimes in a split second, and makes them decide to approach your organisation to do business? Customers are not a uniform entity, and ultimately each customer will have a whole diversity of needs and requirements according to their circumstances. There is, however, a range of split-second decisions any customer will make, sometimes unconsciously, that will influence their purchasing behaviour.

The six satisfaction elements

A company's product or service consists of a number of individual factors known as elements, which separately and collectively directly influence customer satisfaction. Between them, the six elements – known as satisfaction elements – represent every aspect in the purchasing decision of customers.

These six satisfaction elements are as follows:

1. The product or service;
2. Sales;
3. After-sales;
4. Location;
5. Time;
6. Culture.

Figure 1.1 The six satisfaction elements

Each element can be subdivided into factors and considerations. These precisely describe the scope of each element and the considerations that customers bear in mind when they are choosing one product or supplier over another. Having said that, not every factor or consideration is a conscious decision. The psychological/emotional needs a customer experiences when buying a capital-expense product – whether a house, a car, a dining-room suite, a battleship or a combine harvester – will be different from those when buying an everyday or commonplace product such as a loaf of bread, cosmetics, an electric kettle, petrol for the car, or a book. Nonetheless, even a rapid glance through all the factors should show that much more than the product or the sales person can be considered by customers – business or retail – if they compare the total offering provided by each competing supplier.

What actually goes through a customer's mind when deciding to purchase? What attitudes and behaviours make the customer care offered truly excellent?

The answer to this last question is presented in Table 1.1, which lists broad standards of excellence against each satisfaction element factor. Clearly however, since companies and industries are all individual, each will have different expressions of these standards. Your standards and factors will be tailored to your markets and the customers you serve.

Let's start with the product or service element. What might a customer consider?

Does the supplier anticipate my needs? Do I really want or need this product/service? Does it meet my requirements? Is there any risk involved in purchasing this product/service? Does it represent the level of quality I expect for the purchase price? Overall, is it good value for the money?

If you really want a Mercedes and you're looking at a Mini you might find the latter compact and well designed but not expressing the image you wish to convey. How about availability? Do I want it now, or can I wait for a month or two for delivery? In certain industries, for example in car manufacturing, if you see a product that you really like you probably realise that there might be a wait of a month or so for the item you have ordered to arrive. Most will find this acceptable. However, what typically happens with routine purchases, such as a printer? If it is not available in a particular store many customers will go elsewhere. Equally, in certain circumstances the customer will not want to spend funds on a top-end, quality-plus product with all the bells and whistles; they will settle for a cheaper model that does the job adequately.

Let's now look at the sales element. See Table 1.2. What might a customer consider?

This element includes all forms of corporate and product-oriented communication: brochures, web pages, merchandising materials and in-store displays. Do all of these activities reflect the message that a supplier wishes to convey? If for example, brochures are printed on inferior-quality paper and with a poor layout, it will not reflect well on the product or service provider. Your web pages need to download quickly and be customer friendly to use.

The environment where the goods or services are purchased will also have an impact. For example, if the reception area of an

Table 1.1 Satisfaction element 1: product or service

Factor/consideration	Excellence is:
Availability	Immediate availability on or before a negotiated, agreed or promised delivery date. (Overall excellence here is a fast speed-to-market time.)
Product quality	Lifetime zero defects of products.
Service quality	Continually meeting agreed customer requirements for products and services within best-cost limits.
Packaging presentation	Packaging designed to reflect the image of the product and in harmony with other promotional devices. In addition, using packaging consistent with the most responsible current environmental protection standards, and the minimum necessary for hygiene, protection, transportation and storage.
Image	An image that matches reality and is fully in tune with the lifestyle and aspirations of target customers.
Value for money	Ensuring no deception, that is, giving greater (perceived) value than the cost of the purchase.
Fulfilment of expectations	Giving satisfaction in excess of expectations.

office or hotel is scruffy or smells, it will reflect badly on the rest of the facilities. Customers will make a judgement in the first 30 seconds of entering a building.

Table 1.2 Satisfaction element 2: sales

Factor/consideration	Excellence is:
Marketing and merchandising	Honest, legal and decent marketing that is non-intrusive, non-manipulative and non-wasteful, but informative and targeted precisely in terms of market segment and time; researching customers fully so that their needs, preferences and buyer values are understood in fine detail so that corporate strategies can be designed with great accuracy.
Verbal communication	A face-to-face or telephone manner that is attentive, interested, responsive and timely, and which conveys an exact and understandable message that meets the customer's objectives and their need to be heard.
Purchase environment	A wholly welcoming and frictionless environment that, in its temperature, lighting, decor and facilities, is conducive to the easy conduct of business and to making customers feel comfortable emotionally.
Staff	Any staff who have direct contact with the customer should be non-dismissive, responsive, empathetic, trustworthy, knowledgeable, and loyal to the corporate team. They should be well trained, self-reliant and enabled or empowered to act.

Any staff that are in contact with the customer are also being judged. Are there enough of them available to take care of customer queries? Are they approachable? Friendly? Or are they all huddled together having a gossip?

The simplicity and clarity of transaction documentation are important, as is the choice of payment methods (and affordability). Inclusion in a trade or professional association will also give the purchaser the assurance that there is somewhere for them to go should they have a complaint not satisfactorily answered by the supplier they have purchased from.

The inclusion and value of 'purchase variables' such as extended guarantees, training, phased or split deliveries, spares and the availability of additional consumables are also a consideration to a prospective customer.

The after-sales element – See Table 1.3 – includes how responsive staff are in the supplier organisation once the customer has purchased the product or service. This is obviously particularly important with expensive capital expenditure such as cars, computer equipment, battleships and all...

Does the supplier take care of the customer once they have made an initial purchase? For example, do contact centre or customer-care staff have access to a telecom system or software package that identifies the customer who is calling as an existing customer? Do they have immediate access on their PC to the customer's previous purchases?

If the customer has a complaint, does the supplier's staff handle the problem in an effective and efficient way? Are they enabled and empowered to offer a replacement product if the purchased product is faulty?

So how about the location element? See Table 1.4. What might a customer consider?

With the advent of the web and the potential to purchase products or services from anywhere in the world, you would think that location was not so important; but this still is a consideration for a potential customer. Globalised business activities have resulted in call centres being based around the world. Suppliers are now making a point of specifying that their call centre is based in the country

Table 1.3 Satisfaction element 3: after-sales

Factor/consideration	Excellence is:
Maintained interest	Acknowledging and honouring a customer's lifetime value to the company, and not disillusioning loyal customers by failing to acknowledge (and reward) that loyalty; ensuring that the reordering procedure is simple and builds on existing information about customers held by the supplier.
Complaint handling	Enabled and empowered staff responding immediately, courteously, honestly, sympathetically and thoroughly; keeping the customer advised throughout the complaint-management process and using technology as a tool, not as an overlord. (Throughout the sales and after-sales processes it is essential to attune the business to the customer's contact requirements.)

of their target market. The country location of an internet site can sometimes inhibit a purchase. For example, I tried recently to book a hotel room in Indonesia via a US travel agent site. I was unable to finish my purchase as the only option in the address box was to put in a zip code, and living in the UK I was not able to give this.

When it comes to retail outlets it is a different matter. Whoever it was who first replied, 'Location, location, location!' to the question, 'What is important in business?' got it right. Each major retailer has vied with every other for prime sites on high streets and in out-of-town shopping centres. The location of distribution depots, too, is critical to minimising downstream costs and delivery time. Hotels also know how important location is to attracting particular target customers.

Table 1.4 Satisfaction element 4: location

Factor/consideration	Excellence is:
Location	Explaining the location precisely (in text, graphics or verbally) and ensuring that any changes to access roads (layout, names or numbers) or to public transport that serves the area are incorporated in current directions.
Access	Clearly signposting the location, ideally on all access points within a five-minute radius; and ensuring that all the exterior faces of buildings, gateways and drives and all company land reflect the corporate image and convey an empathy with customers.
Security and comfort	Providing adequate lighting, cover and signage to all car parks and entrance ways; ensuring that the internal environment conforms to all relevant health and safety regulations, and that the physical space serves the needs of those using it.
Provision for customers with special needs	Ensuring that nothing discriminates against special-needs groups.
Web-based purchasing	Distribution facilities that enable products to be delivered in the time frame specified on the site.

From the customer's perspective location is not just about the actual position of a building, it is also about convenience of access, security and comfort.

The time element, too – See Table 1.5 – is important for any type of customer, but more so for retail customers at certain times in the working day and also in festive seasons. In this context, how convenient are opening hours? In a hospital environment, time could be of consideration to the customer with regard to how long the snack food trolley is available. Does it stop going around the wards at 6.00 pm when there is a change of staff? For international traders, time is obviously critical as they are driven by a 24-hour clock.

Time can also mean how quickly the supplier can deliver the product or service to the customer. As a supplier you might think that to be able to get your product to a customer in a three-week time frame is 'hot bananas' – a good deal! But if the customer needs the product in the next 10 days your delivery time frame is no good for them.

Once the customer has decided, in principle, on the product or service that they wish to purchase, the culture element within an organisation drives every aspect of customer care. See Table 1.6. Culture is 'the way things are done around here...' If front-line staff are given the tools, equipment and training, and are motivated and supported by their manager, they will offer a quality customer service. This topic is so important that all of Chapter 3 is dedicated to it.

Table 1.5 Satisfaction element 5: time

Factor/consideration	Excellence is:
Business hours	Providing a service according to customers' needs, not according to the presence or absence of competitors.
Applicability and availability of products	Providing a choice of continuously improved products that are relevant to the season and purchase patterns.
Speed of transactions	Pragmatically ensuring that the process is as *short* as customers want it.

Table 1.6 Satisfaction element 6: culture

Factor/ consideration	Excellence is:
Ethics	Being unquestionably legal, non-discriminatory, moral and above board.
Conduct	Being unprejudiced, willingly helpful, objective, even-handed, honest, unimpeachable and authentically customer focused; and learning from constructive criticism.
Internal relationships	Demonstrating fair and balanced treatment of all in the organisation, with no unjustifiable disparities between the highest and lowest members of staff; understanding the concept of co-workers being internal customers; providing opportunities for self- and managed multi-skills development; trusting staff with information and decision-making power; encouraging involvement, team identity and contribution; favouring cross-functional collaboration; and ensuring everyone understands the commitment required to offer excellent customer care.
External relationships	Developing a partnership with suppliers and customers, rather than acting as if discrete parties should be separated by the control exerted by a superior over a subordinate. (Bearing in mind the unprecedented power in the hands of today's customers, it is worth noting that the 'superior' might, in fact, be the customer!) With regard to suppliers, negotiating fair contracts, to develop a 'partnership' arrangement rather than constantly looking for the cheapest bid. Bringing suppliers in at an early product- or service-development phase, so that there is ownership from their point of view to deliver supplies in a cost-effective and timely manner.

In addition to the people element, does the company trade legally and ethically, and is it environmentally responsible? Does it trade equitably with its suppliers? In tender situations, is the company financially sound and prudent?

Reviewing the list above, customers can and do make 'yes' or 'no' subconscious buying decisions, and details such as poor after-sales care *will* impact future sales adversely. There could be other factors that put a potential purchaser off, such as a slow-loading web page or too much additional product information on the page. I personally do not like going on to a black web page screen with flash media. It reminds me of a go-go club with lap dancers, and usually I am not looking to make that type of purchase on the web!

The list of factors above is not comprehensive, but it does lead to three fundamental points:

1. The answers to the questions above are mostly the result of an individual buyer's perception and intuition rather than actuality. Too many negative answers and a customer will believe they will not get the level of customer service and satisfaction they know is their right, and which might be given by an alternative supplier.
2. The process of asking and answering these questions is normally a purely mental exercise for customers. It can happen fast – so fast, in fact, that the customer may not be consciously aware of having posed any questions in their mind. Sometimes we just know when things are 'right' or 'wrong', and this will influence our purchasing decisions.
3. No single element by itself will deliver complete customer satisfaction. This is because each of the six elements contributes something to the overall purchase decision. As I have mentioned above, a brilliant sales element can be tarnished by a poor after-sales element. A perfect service element can be wasted if the location element fails to satisfy. Five of the elements can be in place only to lose ground due to, say, a negatively perceived culture element.

Part of the answer to the question of what makes excellent customer care is that all six satisfaction elements must be developed and delivered concurrently in your organisation to achieve a high quality and depth of care.

Of course, these standards of excellence are not wholly universal. Industrial and retail customers have different expectations. However, they are not so different that the above list cannot serve as a model of high-level care irrespective of your market sector. The best idea is to use the list as a starting point to stimulate your imagination. You can use it with your team, and adapt the copy as you see fit – for example, use during a brainstorming session when you are discussing how to improve the service you offer to your customers.

First contact with an organisation: the 'moment of service truth'

> Here is a simple but powerful rule – always give people more than they expect to get.
>
> *(Nelson Boswell)*

So a customer decides to make first contact with your organisation; it could be by phone, personal visit, e-mail or letter. This is the moment of service truth. How people are greeted by front-line staff in a reception area of an office, hotel or building can influence them. The way that any form of correspondence is dealt with, be it electronically or as hard copy, will also make an impression, as will how people are handled on the telephone.

This comes down to people in the supplier organisation – their approach, their attitude, their willingness to help and make the exchange a positive experience for the customer. How the customer is taken care of from the word go will influence how they feel about your organisation, and whether they wish to continue looking to purchase from you. This applies to both new and existing purchasers. The only judgement a customer can make at this point in time is the other person's behaviour.

This is where care comes into the picture – and it is the vital added ingredient.

> Care comes into the picture during the moment of service truth.

Let's look at 'care' in more detail. What does the word actually mean? The dictionary defines care as, amongst other meanings, 'feeling concern and interest'. So transferring this to the business world we can interpret it as going out of your way to meet your customer's needs. It's also about being proactive and involved rather than passive and withdrawn.

If you are only paying lip service and working to the rules – the quick turn around of food in a fast food restaurant, the correct number of customers through a checkout, answering the appropriate number of calls in a call centre – without providing the personal touch and making the customer feel they are being treated as an individual, then you are not truly caring for them.

Now this does not mean any over-the-top performance or time-consuming activity. Giving them a genuine smile, and/or finding the time to 'read the customer' and offer them what they need at a given moment in time can suffice. In the retail sector, this can range from offering them a small compliment on the colour of jacket they have chosen to purchase, or simply being fast and efficient in packing their merchandise because you can sense the customer is in a rush. On the telephone, when a customer calls a financial institution – say a bank or building society – they often have to go through a lengthy process of data entry and putting in letters or numbers from their password. They may have become agitated by the time they actually get through to the person answering at the call centre. If this person reads their mood, gives them the time to catch their breath, offers a friendly greeting and asks the right questions to find out exactly what they want, they have a good chance of calming the customer down and leaving them with a positive impression of the care they have received. They trust you as a supplier.

> How can you trust the airplane maintenance when they can't wipe the stains off the flip tray?
>
> *(Tom Peters)*

Care is the starting point and a good mnemonic to remember in this context is PERFECT:

P = professional
E = efficient
R = reliable
F = friendly
E = expert
C = caring
T = trustworthy

But when we talk about 'excellence' and 'shining above the competition' there needs to be more than just these basics. You need to exceed expectations and add value wherever you can. A series of small surprises is preferable to an occasional large one. This means 'little and often' rather than 'occasional and extended'. It's a moment in time when a customer feels impressed and happy, and mentally makes a note of the extra care and attention that they receive. So how can you do this?

Exceeding expectations and adding value

Here are a few ideas. It can be a small gesture; for example:

1.   When sending out a brochure, include a 'With compliments' slip with a brief personalised message for the customer.

2. In a hospital, it can be someone taking the time each day to change the water in flower vases.
3. In various shops in Japan you will find a welcome party by the door, and the lift attendant wearing white gloves, and your change returned on a small tray.
4. In a garage it can be that your car is serviced as requested, but when you come to pick it up, the inside of the car has been valeted as an additional service without charge. In contrast, think of how often you have picked up your car after a service and you find the plastic sheet protecting the driver's seat is still there, the seat itself has not been put back to the correct distance for you to drive the car, and the radio is still tuned to a station that the mechanic servicing the car has been listening to! Small details again, but in a negative sense. You at least expect the inside of the car to feel and look the same as when you bought it in to be serviced (subject to there being no repairs needed to the interior when you dropped it into the garage, of course).
5. Personalised tokens such as books of matches, pens or boxes of chocolates imprinted with the name of the guest, member of staff or whoever is the target recipient. This is not a new idea but can still make a big impression. We all like seeing our name in print!

Adding value and exceeding expectations can also mean selectively overwhelming: in other words, doing small things in a big way or looking for little things that make a big difference. Planned spontaneity might seem a contradiction in terms but it is a great technique for exceeding your customer's expectations. For example:

1. You find out that a member of staff or a client has just had a baby. Send them a huge bunch of flowers – so that when other people come to visit the new mother they comment on the floral arrangement. You are sending the message that 'You are important to me!'
2. The classic added value in hotels: putting flowers on the food tray, chocolates on the bed, fruit in the room – and a pair of

scales so you can weigh yourself once you have eaten all the added-value goodies!

3. Also in a hotel, not needing to check in at reception. Instead a receptionist comes to your room for registration purposes.

4. Cleaners in hotels not pushing against your door with the vacuum cleaner first thing in the morning! Hotel staff saying hello to you in the corridor. The porter chatting to you as you go to your room: 'Have you travelled far?' 'Good choice of hotel!'

5. The wedding arranger who organises a couple's wedding sends them a bottle of wine on their first anniversary.

And finally:

6. In the office, there is no money for a salary increase, so instead you are given a bigger job title – Sales Director, etc! Obviously this is not really an added-value service to you, just a common ploy that firms use when budget is tight.

> Small gestures make a big difference.

So there you go. Customers make a quick mental judgement on whether they want to buy your product or service based on satisfaction elements. They then expect a fundamental level of care by a supplier as a given, and you can really shine and offer excellence in service by doing that little bit more. What's stopping you? It doesn't hurt. It's not like many things – mandatory, prohibited or taxed! It just takes that little bit of thought, effort and, of course, a positive attitude.

Key questions

- How do you as an organisation stack up against the six satisfaction elements?
- Are you and your team just offering the basic level of care?
- What can you do to make sure you and your team can make a difference to the level of service a customer is offered?
- How can you add value and 'wow' the customer?

2

Getting to know your customer's needs and requirements

> Just when I thought I knew all the answers, life started asking me all the wrong questions.
>
> *(Anonymous)*

Introduction

So how do you know what your customer's needs and requirements are? Let me share a scenario with you, and see if it rings any bells with you.

I shop at a particular supermarket because it caters for people that are single or have a small family; you can buy small packets of produce and fresh food goods, you don't have to buy the jumbo-sized packs of cereals, nuts, potatoes or whatever that you find in other supermarkets. The pricing structure of this supermarket is higher than its competitors: they trade on the importance of quality (perhaps you know who I am talking about now!). But in a quick reckoning as we are a small family, I have always thought that I would be throwing away large quantities of perishable goods from cheaper supermarket purchases, so the cost at the end of the day would be pretty comparable. There are other small considerations that go through my mind as well; for example, only being able to purchase a particular product (often own brand) at this supermarket that hooks me in.

Not that I am being that scientific about the target audience of customers who use this supermarket, but a cursory glance at other people I have seen using this brand of store indicates that their profile is single or small families.

Periodically I do not have time to get to a store, so I use their web-based company to purchase my weekly shop. The site is easy to use, performs as most supermarket sites do, and reminds you each time of your purchases from your previous shop with them. The delivery is 9 times out of 10 on time, and even if the van driver is a few minutes late they deduct the delivery charge from the bill. The produce comes in excellent condition, slightly chilled, and when you open up the bag you find a small added-value gesture, a thank-you note with a bar of Green and Blacks chocolate inside. There is also a special offer deal included for the next purchase.

What could be better than this? The ease and convenience of being able to shop at the supermarket of your choice, place the order when it is convenient to you, and delivered to your door at an agreed time slot. Now this is completely subjective, with me as the customer, but I still only use the web-based service periodically. Why is this?

Because when I open up the shopping bags I find jumbo-sized versions of my orders. When you click on a product there is often not a choice in the size of product that you buy. In a split second I feel duped. They have 'got me' as a customer, and they are going to maximise the purchase to make more money. I resent this. It is contradictory to the very reason I have chosen this supermarket in the first place.

In the meantime, after my initial purchase with the web-based company I get regular mailings by e-mail and direct marketing flyers through the post giving me offers such as £x off my next purchase if I place an order by a particular date. They also send sweet postcards saying 'We're missing you' as if from a personal friend. All good after-sales activities, which, let's face it, must have a built-in cost.

Where is the missing link in this scenario? The web-based company is spending funds on me with their after-sales activities, but not getting to the root of my dissatisfaction. They are not finding out why I am not purchasing again.

So how do we know what our customers really think about us, rather than our own perception of what they think of us, and our products and services? It comes down to research.

What should the company and you as a manager be looking for during any research process?

1. Do we deliver what we promise?
2. Are we delivering services that are really important to the customer, or are we wasting resources that could be utilised in a more profitable way?
3. Is there a true added-value service offered by all in the business, or is it a bit hit and miss?
4. Do we understand the different types of customers in our marketplace?
5. In turn, do we focus on superior service in areas that matter most to a range of different customers?
6. Do we know how they want to work with us in the future?
7. Do we know how we as a business can help them?
8. Do we understand the difference between customer satisfaction and customer loyalty?
9. How do we stack up against our competitors?

Where to gather your information

Let's look at three routes you can take to find out this information: by investigating complaints, by proactively undertaking various types of research, and by benchmarking.

First, looking at complaints.

> Man invented language in order to satisfy his deep need to complain.
>
> *(Lily Tomlin, 1939–)*

Gaining customer feedback from complaints

The harsh reality is that often customers don't bother to let you know they are unhappy with the product or service you provide. They just go elsewhere, spreading the negative word about your company. So if a customer does complain, welcome the contact, as it gives you the opportunity to investigate and put things right, and even build more business with them if you handle the situation well and to their satisfaction. Chapter 6 is dedicated to this topic , but as we are talking about gathering information to find out more about your customers' needs and requirements, I would like to look at this particular aspect in more detail here.

First of all, you need to make sure that the customer has ease of access to contact the pertinent department if they have a complaint. As a consumer you can often find that you call a company and the automated telephone menu system doesn't even offer you the option of a customer service department, or how you can make a complaint!

So, if your department is the primary contact point for complaint handling and problem resolution, make sure that there is not a long-winded method on your website to do this. Also put a free or local-rate customer services number on your invoices as well as the website.

Be wary of creating contracts with punitive termination penalties for customers who wish to cancel their contract. Gyms and leisure facilities are particularly prone to doing this – making a customer give at least four months' notice to cancel their contract, even when the customer has been using the facility for several years. By doing this they might squeeze a small amount of extra revenue from the customer, but will often leave a bad taste in the customer's mouth, and the resolution to never use that particular chain of gyms or leisure facilities again. The customer will also not be particularly willing to give you feedback as to why they are leaving, which could be invaluable in terms of finding out what needs to be improved.

> Be wary of creating contracts with punitive termination penalties.

As you will see when you read Chapter 6, there needs to be transparency and openness about problem areas that are occurring, and often there will be cross-functional activity to move things forward and resolve the situation (for example, getting together different departments or teams who are affected by a particular issue: customer service, product development, manufacturing, finance, etc). If you are responsible for a customer service department or a contact or call centre, managers at a more senior level need to be kept informed of the issues you have to deal with and resolve. Senior management can't be kept in an ivory tower and be blissfully ignorant of problems that are occurring within your company. The whole purpose of gathering information, be it feedback via a complaint or through market research, is to forewarn companies and give them the opportunity to prepare and plan – to be forearmed – with precision, and to prevent wasted effort.

Complaints come to you, but the proactive approach to finding out your customers' needs and requirements is through research and also comparison with your competition: benchmarking.

Research

There is no question that the popularity of research in the form of surveys is on the rise. You can't go anywhere without having to complete a customer feedback questionnaire or survey; they are in hotels, planes, restaurants, garages, everywhere. If you currently use research, how do you know if you are using the correct methodology to gather information?

Any market research is only as good as, first of all, the methods used; second, the extent, detail and honesty of the data collected; third, the regularity with which the research is conducted; fourth, how truly representative of a total population a sample of respondents is; fifth, how expertly the collected data are analysed; sixth, how willing the company or manager who has commissioned the research is to share the results and conclusions internally; and seventh, how willing the manager or company is to respond to the conclusions. In a small team or department it can usually be comparatively straightforward to implement recommendations that emerge from research data, if these do not encroach on other departments or teams' territory. In many organisations, however, it can be a real battle to persuade the various internal groups – many motivated by self-serving and competing interests – that enhanced customer service is the measure by which their company is judged and used. There is more about this thorny topic of persuading our internal colleagues to come around to our point of view in Chapter 5.

What are the different research methods you can use?

Research methods

Here are a list and brief explanation of the most common methods of researching customers and markets, starting with those that middle managers are most likely to find useful. The first four methods are relatively quick and easy to set up; the remaining types usually require greater investment in time and money and are more likely to be used company-wide.

Mystery shoppers

These are people contracted to a company to be 'sensory representatives in the field', and trained to record their experiences objectively as a real-life customer. Mystery shopping is an invaluable source of data and is a common way of gathering mass information cost effectively.

Opinion/perception surveys

Conducted as face-to-face, online, telephone or postal interviews, these surveys are a useful way of actively gathering mass information. They can, however, suffer from what has been called 'interviewee inertia', that is, the state of boredom and indifference caused by being asked to respond to yet another questionnaire. Therefore interviewers must be trained adequately, the questionnaire must be designed expertly and the exercise must be funded properly to ensure a sufficiently robust set of data.

Customer comment (and guarantee) cards

These are a passive way of collecting information. As the number of customers who are prepared to fill out a responsive card is likely to be only a small percentage of all customers, the data might not be statistically relevant. Again, however, some issues – which might need deeper probing – can be revealed. The response rate can be increased by simply making the cards visually appealing and by attaching an incentive to their completion. But it must be borne in mind that some people will return only a positive comment because they believe they will not receive their reward for a negative one. The same comments apply to online equivalents.

Personal meetings by you or a member of your team

These are essential, but as the meetings are likely to be sporadic and cursory the inadequacies of such personal sampling must be balanced by data gathered by other means.

Customer focus groups

These are a productive way of identifying customers' opinions about a specific issue. These small groups – intensive and facilitator-led question and brainstorming sessions – can be highly revealing, but as they concentrate on only a narrow horizon they can be a time-consuming and expensive way of gathering data statistically relevant in depth and breadth. However, the results can provide useful pointers that you can choose to validate by other means.

Market research

Market research data give only half the story; customer research data give the rest. There are significant differences between how these two sets of data should be used. Market research measures customers in groups and gives aggregate – or big picture – results aimed at helping a company determine customer base-influencing strategies. Customer research emphasises the individuality of customers and aims to influence a company's internal satisfaction process.

Customer panels

A customer panel consists of a number of people who reflect the typical profile of a market segment, acting as a company's 'guinea pigs'. Their perceptions and opinions as test customers considering a broad range of issues are a valuable source of subjective data.

Critical incident analyses

These require staff, skilled in non-threatening interrogative techniques and report writing, to record customers' feelings when they have been particularly pleased or displeased by service received. The written report must be classified (under an 'incident type') and used to stimulate action, to justify the exercise.

Customer interview videos

By its nature, this method also is likely to be time consuming, expensive and limited by personal sampling. However, the advantage of capturing interviews on film is the chance it gives to analyse body language – hence the emotional content – in conjunction with the interviewees' verbal responses.

Product user groups

These are useful forums in which to capture opinions and modification ideas which real customers believe will offer them increased value for money. The key is for the manufacturer or service provider to link with the groups without appearing to take them over or use the association for ulterior and hidden reasons. Trust and openness can produce a genuine two-way flow of data.

Using more than one research method

Obtaining regular and substantial feedback from customers is crucial for reducing complaints, aiding customer service, making improvements and positioning the company and its products precisely.

It is a common and false assumption that just one or two feedback methods are all that are needed to get a clear, and continuing, picture of customers' needs and opinions. No single communication channel will be wholly sufficient, as every research method contains its own unavoidable potential to corrupt the quality of data. It is therefore best to use all means of feedback to smooth out the anomalies caused by single processes. The sheer wealth of resulting data can be overwhelming (and the cause of another set of problems to analyse it), but it does allow the simultaneous collection of big-picture and individual customer information to inform strategic (executive) and tactical (operational) decisions.

> You need more than one or two methods to get a clear and continuing picture of customers' needs and opinions.

Conducting effective surveys

There are of course many reasons for doing surveys. Using the results as good PR is one of the most common. How many departments or companies can resist splashing out with headlines such as '97 per cent of our customers are satisfied'? Such claims can, however, backfire. An increasingly sceptical public, not to mention sometimes wary colleagues, are more and more likely not to be bowled over by your triumph and to subject you to third-degree questioning: what does this mean; who did you ask; what exactly did you ask? And they are right to do so. Too often surveys are constructed unprofessionally and the results used too laxly. At worst, this can bring your whole business into disrepute; at best, benefits are likely to be limited.

This need not be so. If surveys are carefully planned and executed they can yield extremely useful results, and may finally even lead to some stimulating headlines, although this should never be the main aim of the survey.

The starting point should always be: why exactly do you want to do a survey? Be clear in your mind about what you really want to find out and why. Also ask yourself whether a survey is the best way to find out what you want. Customer surveys, whether on paper, online or on the phone, must be quick and simple. If not, people will either not start the survey or will drop out halfway through. This format limits the number and type of questions you can ask, as well as the amount of information you can glean. For more complex issues, other types of research, such as group discussions, would probably be more effective.

Let's stick for now to the simple customer survey that is typically found in hotels and on planes, or which is administered online or on the phone after a client has used your service. We have all seen hundreds of examples of these, so when you're writing the survey, don't forget how you feel yourself when you're asked to complete a survey. If the survey is boring, too complicated, the same as all the surveys you've ever seen, too long, etc, how likely are you to complete it? If you think the company is going to ignore your comments, again, how likely are you to spend time giving your opinion?

The way the survey is presented and its context within your service are therefore important. Your interaction with the customer before the survey must indicate clearly that you are interested in their views, or you cannot expect a good response. The particularly annoying statement, 'Your opinion really matters to us,' will generally be counterproductive, unless you have shown already or can show that this is true. Why not, for example, include at the start of the survey a very brief example of how customer feedback has helped improve your service in the past? 'Customers told us the swimming pool closed too early. It is now open until midnight.' 'Customers asked for Fairtrade coffee for breakfast. Come and have a cup after you've completed this survey.'

Once you have the customer's attention, make sure you ask the right questions. Do you want to know about a particular service or product or do you want to find out about overall customer satisfaction? In the case of a hotel, for example, if you want to use the result to improve your service, it may well be most effective to ask a few questions about one or two particular aspects (the room, the restaurant) for three months and then switch to one or two other particular aspects. This will enable you to delve a little into each area, without creating a questionnaire that is too long or boring.

Consider too the format you will use for the answers. Typically surveys use a five-point scale, with 5 as excellent and 1 as poor. In many cases, however, this does not fit the customer's experience or provide an accurate measurement of their views. Part of a survey I picked up recently is shown in Table 2.1.

This will give some data and will perhaps highlight anything that is severely wrong, but will it really be of use if you want to improve your service?

First, a customer could say the cleanliness of the bathroom was good, but was it as good as they were expecting or were they actually a bit disappointed? Would a different scale be better?

Table 2.1 Example of hotel survey

Your room	5 excellent	4 very good	3 good	2 not very good	1 poor
How would you rate:					
– cleanliness of bedroom					
– cleanliness of bathroom					
– television					
– lighting					
– heating/air conditioning					
– overall satisfaction with your room					
Any comments:					

Second, a customer may not have used the television or the heating or air conditioning. A not-applicable column should always be added or customers may feel frustrated and your results may be skewed. More importantly, will the answers help you think about actions to improve your service? It is possible they will, but in most cases they will not, as they do not address the key issues.

What you are probably aiming to find out is if the customer was so happy with their room that they will come back to your hotel again or recommend it to their friends and colleagues. These questions do not enable you to do this. A customer could answer 'good' or even 'very good' to all the questions above and still not be happy enough to return. Cleanliness, lighting, etc are important factors in satisfaction, but they are not the only ones, and not even necessarily the most important ones. Most customers primarily want a room that enables them to sleep well and wake up refreshed. However clean the bathroom is, if an ice machine is outside your door or the window rattles, you are unlikely to sleep well and therefore unlikely to be truly satisfied with your stay. An alternative format for the survey, as shown in Table 2.2, might give you more accurate and more useful feedback.

This kind of survey may give you some pointers about what you could improve. It can be dangerous, though, to rely solely on this or any other single source of information. Using the survey results, you could organise some face-to-face interviews or some group discussions with customers and delve much more deeply into what they think and what they are looking for.

Check too that you are surveying the right people and that you spread your net wide enough. Many people may be involved in the sale of your product or service. Imagine you are selling car insurance. Your customer may be an agent, who then sells the policy to the end user. Increasingly, you may sell direct to the policy holder, but even then other people (the driver's spouse, children, etc) may well be involved. Even in the hotel case, a company, rather than the guests themselves, may take the booking decision. Take time therefore to check that you are surveying the right people, and that you include all the relevant groups of people, as well as asking the right questions.

Table 2.2 Alternative format of hotel survey

Your room	exceptional	above average	average	below my expectations	not applicable
First impression					
Overall condition of the room					
– please note any areas that were below your expectations					
Amenities					
– please note any areas that were below your expectations					
How was your night's sleep?					
– please mention anything we could do to improve it next time					

Online surveys

Surveys such as the hotel example above can easily be organised online. The problem is not so much the survey as persuading people to take the time to fill it in. Incentives are worth looking at (a chance to win a case of champagne, a free night's accommodation, etc), provided you choose them carefully to appeal to your target audience. The advantages of online surveys are clear. They are quick to set up; the results can be analysed rapidly; the questionnaire can be more flexible than a written one (the questionnaire can automatically skip questions as appropriate). On the other hand, remember that you are still, despite huge growth in internet usage, most like to receive responses from younger and more highly educated people than the population at large. This may not be a problem, depending on who you are surveying, but in some cases it means you will end up with results that do not reflect your customers as a whole.

Benchmarking

Finally, there is benchmarking. This is a process you can use to find out how various aspects of your processes compare with your peers or competitors. By measuring your performance you can have an accurate indicator of what needs to improve. By measurement you can see where you are now, and how high to set the performance bar.

As with survey research, it is important to make sure you know why you are benchmarking and be clear about what you want to get out of it. In the case of customer service, there have been cases when companies have paid too much attention to what their competitors are doing and adopted a copycat approach rather than developing their own way of doing business, with its own advantages and benefits. Benchmarking can also lead too easily to a ticking-the-box approach, where everything seems rosy provided a telephone call is answered within three rings. Having said all this, an intelligent approach to benchmarking can yield very helpful results.

The first requirement for successful benchmarking is to decide who you are going to compare yourself with. The obvious answer may be your competitors. By looking at their processes and outcomes in as much detail as possible, you may be able to identify areas of weakness in your own operation. It is not necessary, however, nor is it always desirable only to measure yourself against others in your own industry. Sometimes stepping outside and looking at how other industries perform similar tasks may shed more light on your own operation.

> During benchmarking activities, sometimes look at how other industries perform similar tasks to yours.

A frequently quoted story concerns the American Automobile Association (AAA), who apparently learnt by benchmarking themselves against Domino's Pizza. AAA customers had begun to wonder why it was that that Domino's could make and deliver a pizza within 30 minutes, but it often took AAA much longer to respond to a call-out. AAA looked into the situation and agreed that they should be able to get a repair vehicle to their customers at least as quickly. Similarly, Honda in the UK have recently sought to benchmark themselves against other leading brands outside the car industry, for example Apple or John Lewis, as these companies represent their customers' perception of reliable and trusted brands. In other words, by benchmarking themselves against companies in a different sector, both AAA and Honda were able to identify where to make tangible improvements.

Benchmarking can also be used internally to compare performance between departments or teams and find areas for improvement. Again, it is important to take care that this does not become a mere box-ticking exercise, but that it is a genuine tool for driving the business forward.

Once you have decided who you are going to compare yourself with, you should be clear about what you are going to compare. Typical customer service measures include:

- **the proportion of returning customers;**
- **the time taken to fulfil an order;**
- **the proportion of returned goods;**
- **the number of complaints;**
- **the time taken to answer the phone.**

The measures you choose should suit your business and you should choose them with an eye to how you can use the results to give your customers a better experience. There is clearly no point in answering the phone quickly if this is at the expense of a more important activity.

Depending on your business, you may also be limited by the amount of information available on your competitors. If no data are available, for example from trade associations or surveys, to compare your business with, you will need to be more inventive and create your own performance levels, perhaps in cooperation with your customers, who, after all, are the people you are trying to satisfy.

Perhaps this is no bad thing. After a period of great popularity, the apparent benefits of benchmarking as a form of research are increasingly being criticised. If you are not careful, benchmarking can lead to complacency: you are as good as your competitors, so why worry? In most circumstances too, benchmarking does not reveal the secret of success of your competitors; and it will rarely tell you how to outperform them. For that, some of the other types of research outlined above, as a basis for brainstorming and in-house work, are more likely to give you the creative edge you are looking for.

Key questions

- Do you use the feedback you get from complaints to improve your customer service?
- Are you using the right method of research to find out what you need to know?
- Are your surveys quick and easy to complete, and are you getting enough responses to make good judgements?
- Do you really think you are asking the right questions on your survey forms?
- How much valuable information are you gathering from a benchmarking visit? Was it really worth it?

Creating the environment for customer care to flourish

If you believe in me, I'll believe in you.
(Lewis Carroll, Through the Looking Glass, *1872)*

Introduction

Excellence in customer care cannot happen on its own. It is up to you as manager to create the environment or culture for your reports to truly flourish and be motivated not only to be competent and add value wherever they can, but also to contribute more in terms of ideas for improvement. This could be in relation to operational matters, the service offered or the products you produce. This will involve a review and awareness of attitudes, behaviour and work methodologies. It involves everyone in your team or department – including you – and needs everyone's commitment.

What do we mean by the word 'culture'? As I have already mentioned, it is 'the way things are done around here', or the way people behave towards each other in any business environment. In teams or departments, the culture is usually determined by the team leader or manager. We are not talking about the culture of your organisation here. I acknowledge that it will have an enormous impact on your ability to be heard and to achieve your objectives. However, as the manager, you can create a motivating environment for your reports where everyone is heard, nobody feels rejected or left out, and everyone's opinion is valued.

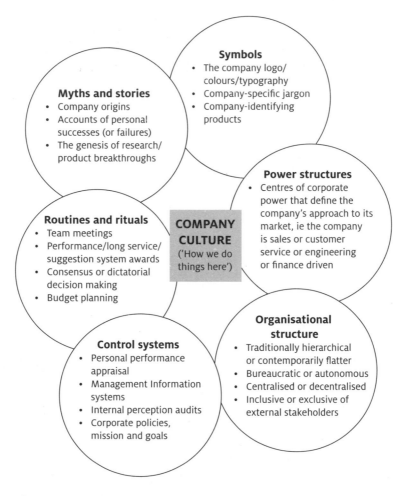

Figure 3.1 What makes a company's culture?

In your team or department there will be certain occasions when you need to put together a project team or task force. This could be when you want to introduce a new service or, if pertinent, a new product or revised documentation. You cannot base your throughput of work solely on this form of activity.

There also needs to be evolutionary activity going on, based on continuously examining work flows, quality improvements and problem-solving activities. The Japanese, who excel at this form of activity, call this Kaizen. The word literally means 'change and good', which in business terms translates as 'continuous improvement'.

A person can make improvements once if they try. They will only make improvements continually if they care. So it is your job to create an environment where team members feel needed, supported and valued as individuals. How do you go about this?

You cannot force people to be customer focused, add value and come up with ideas for improvement. You need to create an environment where people can have a sense of pride in their work, where they can feel that their ideas and suggestions are listened to, that feedback is given, not only for those ideas that are implemented but also when they are not.

Reward and recognition are obviously part of the equation, but so also is the right to take risks and experiment without fear of retribution if things go wrong. Personal development and multi-skilling are other vital ingredients that make people feel that your organisation cares about them as individuals, and which in turn will encourage them to want to contribute more.

Your style of leadership and the creation of a framework to monitor and measure performance can make all the difference. This chapter will explore both of these elements.

Style of leadership

'Command and control' style of leadership is pertinent in certain highly charged situations, for example in the fire brigade when firefighters are going into a burning building. Likewise when a surgeon is undertaking an operation, clear concise instructions are vital.

In less charged situations than these your style of leadership should be far more consultative and involving of others. Your role should be to coach and facilitate those reporting to you to come up with their own ideas as to how to tackle their workload or problem solve. In a snapshot you will see in the illustration below the key foundation skills that are required to be an effective manager.

Looking specifically at how to motivate your team, it is vital that your leadership style encompasses the following:

1. visibility and openness;
2. the creation of a customer-focused environment;
3. the robustness of information you supply;
4. the development of a learning environment;
5. enabling and empowering team members;
6. a 'no blame' approach.

Figure 3.2 Management skills

Visibility and openness

We have already explored the need for customer-facing staff to offer not only value-for-money service, but also to go that extra mile whenever they can. For you to be constantly up-to-date with the marketplace you should be out there in your department or team, seeing and hearing what is happening, being a visible manager. This is not to find fault and endlessly check what front-line staff are doing, but to be there to encourage and support them in offering the best possible service. You will also be able to see at first hand where problem areas might be occurring, and bring these areas to people's attention at team meetings, if others have not already flagged the problem areas themselves.

The film producer Sam Goldwyn once said, 'I don't want yes men around me. I want everyone to tell the truth even if it costs them their job!'

Needless to say, this approach would not encourage openness. So what do we mean by this word? It is about removing fear, causing everyone's opinion to be valued, including minority views. There should be an open acknowledgement that in everyday working activity, problems exist. It is important that they are not swept under the carpet or simply put through the 'rumour network', which will result in them being addressed in a fire-fighting way.

Unless you know what the problem areas are, how can you start to address them? Chapter 6 goes into detail about this thorny area.

> Openness is about removing fear, causing everyone's opinion to be valued, including minority views.

The creation of a customer-focused environment

Let's move on to looking at what you personally can do, and the techniques you can use, to flag to your team that they need to be customer focused.

If you work on a shop floor or at front of house or in a public area where you interface with members of the public, should a customer approach you for advice while you are talking to one of your team, stop what you are doing and give the customer attention. We have all experienced the frustration of being in a shop, approaching a manager or supervisor who is giving instructions or talking to a member of their team, for both parties to completely ignore us as a customer until they have finished their conversation. This does not make you feel wanted as a customer. The same applies on the telephone. If you are in conversation with a work colleague and a customer calls, they get priority.

Even if you work in a department that does not directly interface with the customer, you need to be aware of the key customers of your organisation. So mention who these are at team meetings, what they buy from your organisation, and emphasise that these are the people who pay your salary!

Visual aids – such as posters or flyers – emphasising the importance of the customer should be put on display in prominent positions. And if you have a notice board, any press cuttings about your customers or news about developments in your business with them could be displayed.

Circulate customer success stories via e-mail to those people you regularly have contact with in other parts of the organisation, to keep them up-to-date with customer developments and news.

The robustness of information you supply

Who you are as an organisation and where you wish to be in the future – in other words, the vision and strategies of the organisation – need to be communicated on a regular basis, and must excite people by connecting to their values.

The word 'inform' does not just mean to tell people information, but to put it into context. It is important to ensure that your team members not only understand the facts but also the implications and the context of the information that you are supplying.

Should you, for example, be presenting facts and figures, then your team may need to have been given basic financial training in order to be able to interpret the information. Statistics also need to be produced in a user-friendly way.

Very often I visit organisations that display their results for staff to see. The statistical information will often be produced in figure format, and laid out on paper that has started to curl over and look rather like tired cheese sandwiches. This is quite a turn-off. In contrast, on a client site that I visited in the USA, the company president had produced all the pertinent information with regard to shipping, distribution and production in a graph format and had put small personal observations against some of the pie charts. This really brought all the information to life and made far more sense to the staff who were reading it.

Bear in mind that information is rather like a lift. It only works well if it goes up as well as down. It is the manager's responsibility to ensure that the information does not come up through filters and down through megaphones!

The development of a learning environment

> Learning is not compulsory. Neither is survival.
>
> *(W Edward Deming)*

The development of a learning environment covers many of the factors we are exploring in this checklist. The old business world was about productivity – doing the same thing over and over again, but more cheaply. The new business world is about giving people in-depth knowledge to do their job, and about maximising imagination, asking the questions that your competitors have missed and exploiting the answers creatively and fast.

So to get your team to think more creatively you need to expand their tasks and activities, and in doing this enable and empower them to make decisions for themselves. On certain occasions, if they do not know what they have to do, communication from you is sufficient. If people are a little hesitant, then motivation certainly comes into the equation. In various instances people do not have the skill sets to take on a task, so they need to be developed and trained. Let's explore how you can go about developing others.

There are many ways of learning, developing and growing. Personal development should not be considered as something that happens only on a training course, for in reality some of the most effective ways of learning can come from undertaking day-to-day activities.

Your team members' training-need requirements will result from the appraisal and coaching process, and other ad hoc performance-related issues. So how should you go about developing others?

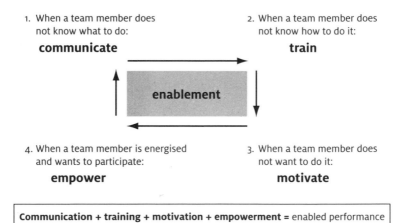

Figure 3.3 The enablement equation

Learning and development resources

There are a variety of learning and development resources that can be used:

Self-learning through the use of:
- distance learning, computer-based training, CD ROMs and DVDs;
- intranet and internet;
- knowledge portals.

'Experiential' learning and development:
- on-the-job training;
- 'sitting with Nelly';
- undertaking specific tasks and projects;
- job rotation;
- secondment, ie attachment to another team or department for an agreed period of time;
- organising a 'best practice' benchmarking visit.

Guidance:
- coaching;
- mentoring.

Formal training; for example, in-house or public-course training programmes.

There should be some form of learning resource library either in your department or in the HR or training department. If there is not, create one yourself to include the latest range of publications in your industry sector, and best-practice customer-care case studies from a variety of industry sectors around the world. Let's face it, people have similar customer service issues regardless of the sector they are in, and we can all learn a lot from other organisations' experiences.

> That is what learning is. You suddenly understand something you have understood all your life, but in a new way.
>
> *(Doris Lessing, author, 1919–)*

A learning environment encourages every form of personal development, and most blue-chip organisations have learning resources in place for many forms of leisure activities.

Enabling and empowering team members

> Tell me and I will forget,
> Show me and I may remember,
> Involve me and I will understand.

(Chinese proverb)

Enabling and empowering your team members is best practice. The issue I constantly find in organisations is that there is no understanding or agreement of what true enablement and empowerment actually mean. All too often team members feel that management 'want things yesterday' without consideration for current workload or work priorities, and no consideration for internal and external customer needs and requirement. Team members feel 'dumped on', without support or guidance. They flounder because they don't have adequate resources and don't know where to go to gather information. In turn, I have also heard the comment from someone I interviewed during a research assignment in a company, 'My manager is very good at delegating; she always find someone to blame when things go wrong!' Now all of this is not going to encourage your team to welcome being enabled or empowered.

The reality is that, as a manager, you will inevitably need to pass work to members of your team. If done properly, this will not only reduce your own workload but will also give others the opportunity to develop their own capabilities and broaden their skill sets. This can be highly motivational, as people can feel valued for the contribution that they are able to make. If people feel an enhanced sense of worth, they will have a greater sense of commitment to their working activities. When people are communicated with effectively, given skills, tools and responsibility, they thrive.

Prior to delegating, you need to be clear in your own mind what the main objective of your job is and how you should be spending your time, and then see what tasks might be done by someone else. It could be that a member of your team has a good graphic eye. For example, do you always have to be the person that creates the PowerPoint visuals in your reports, or could one of your team do them? An individual could also have more technical expertise than you at a particular phase of a project, and this will fast-track the overall delivery time of the assignment. Bearing in mind the need for continuous development of your team members' skill sets, there could often be occasions when you could get a junior team member to stand in for you and, by doing so, let them gain experience. Meetings often provide a good opportunity for this approach.

To enable and empower is to move from giving instructions on how to do a particular task or activity to giving the team or individual the power to act on their own initiative, and take responsibility for how to tackle it. It's an obvious idea: the people closest to the work understand it best, they are the experts, they know what the customer wants because they work with them all the time.

Empowering your team is not to hand them company command and control. That, and ultimate decision-making authority, must remain with you as a manager, but it should enable them to make and act on local decisions that influence their own work. This means that each team member and team must be given a defined arena of functional freedom within which they can exercise their knowledge and skills. For example, in a call centre for roadside recovery, if a customer has broken down and is waiting for the mechanic to turn up, they are in a town centre and it is raining, the customer-care operative might suggest that the customer go to a local coffee shop to get a drink and something to eat up to a certain financial limit, and this will be paid for by the recovery company. This is a small gesture, but adding value to their service. As a broad rule of thumb, front-line staff should be given guidelines with regard to whether they can offer discounts to customers, and in what circumstances. They should not have to come to you each time for clearance.

Decisions or actions that potentially take an individual or group across their arena boundary will, of course, be subject to your clearance, and they will be aware of this. But inside the arena the team or individual must be free, that is, enabled and empowered, to operate according to the agreed limits.

How do you go about creating an enabled and empowered environment where team members can take the initiative in this way?

How you delegate depends very much on the level of experience and ability of the person involved or the maturity of your team, and there are going to be certain activities where it is not possible to enable or empower staff. This could be in relation to legislative requirements, financial control mechanisms, legal constraints, security or specific standards that need to be adhered to for quality-control purposes.

Looking at the different levels above, there are occasions when you simply tell a group or an individual what needs to happen – a straightforward instruction. It makes common sense, though, that the more people feel involved and included in the decision-making process, the more they will feel motivated to think laterally and creatively to come up with ideas themselves as to how a task should be tackled and implemented.

Figure 3.4 shows how you can move from a directive to a more participative approach, facilitating others to take things forward.

Prerequisites for successful delegation

Your attitude and support as a manager during the delegation process are key to successful empowerment.

Team members need:

1. clearly stated objectives for what they have to achieve and specific reasons why;
2. an exact description of the quality standard to be achieved;
3. a realistic time frame, and access to budget should they require this;
4. guidelines in place as to the scope of empowerment that is being exercised and where the limitations lie;
5. clarification of where the team member or team can source information or resources;
6. appropriate authority, with arrangements made for them to receive it;

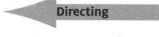

Directing	Facilitating
• Tell team members what processes and tools to use	• Suggest processes and tools – let team members choose
• Provide answers to team members' questions	• Coach team members to find own answers
• Take direct actions to ensure team makes good decisions	• Help team make their own decisions by facilitating discussion process
• Direct team meetings and progress	• Observe team meetings and monitor progress
• Provide resources; link team members with the rest of the organisation	• Reinforce team members' ability to find their own resources, make their own links
• Intervene in team activities frequently to keep team on track	• Intervene only when team members are not making any progress
• Teach team members basic tools of project management and team building	• Teach team members advance tools; reinforce use of basic tools

Figure 3.4 Directing and facilitating

7. discretionary powers to do the job;
8. your assurance that you will represent their interests and keep the predators at bay;
9. to know what kind of progress reports are wanted, by when and how often;
10. your identification of the conditions under which they should contact you for assistance.

You have to bear in mind that, initially at least, it can take you more time to delegate than to do the activity yourself.

It is important to not keep checking up – leave team members time to think and reach their own decisions. If someone comes to you for advice, try to encourage them to think through the problem themselves, by asking them a series of open questions about the issue concerned.

And above all else, do not take credit for other people's work – acknowledge their input, and celebrate how they have tackled a particular task, and the results they have achieved.

Thinking at an individual level, sometimes it is obvious who you should delegate a task to. But equally well you might have to think in more detail about the range of skills and competencies in your team.

What different people in your team might contribute

It is important to recognise that any team is only as good as the sum of its members. Each member is different but important. Team members don't need to be all the same. In fact, to be successful a team needs a mix of people, personalities and skills. An individual may, and often does, exhibit strong tendencies towards multiple roles. Certainly in small teams an individual can play more than one role.

There has been interesting and extensive research undertaken by R Meredith Belbin initially at Henley Management College into the different roles that people might adopt in a team. Table 3.1 provides a brief resumé of the team types that were identified during the research project, which has been updated and fine-tuned over the years.

Using this behavioural tool, how can you best utilise your direct reports when you are thinking about delegating a particular task or activity to a member of your team or setting up a project? Let's look at a few of the characteristics identified above.

The term 'plant' was used by Belbin because this type of team member appeared to 'sit in the corner' and not interact a lot, rather like a house plant.

Plants are creative, unorthodox and good at generating ideas. For in-depth problem solving or at the start of a new project, they are an excellent resource to use. They often bear a strong resemblance to the caricature of the 'absent-minded professor', and are not always that good at communicating ideas to others. So you need to tap into their creativity, and draw information from them by using the facilitating open-questioning techniques described in Chapter 4.

Table 3.1 The nine team roles

Role and description	Team role contribution
Plant	Creative, imaginative, unorthodox, solves difficult problems.
Resource investigator	Extrovert, enthusiastic, communicative. Explores opportunities. Develops contacts.
Coordinator	Mature, confident, a good chairperson. Clarifies goals, promotes decision making, delegates well.
Shaper	Challenging, dynamic, thrives on pressure. Has the drive and courage to overcome obstacles.
Monitor evaluator	Sober, strategic and discerning. Sees all options. Judges accurately.
Teamworker	Cooperative, mild, perceptive and diplomatic. Listens, builds, averts friction, calms the waters.
Implementer	Disciplined, reliable, conservative and efficient. Turns ideas into practical actions.
Completer	Painstaking, conscientious, anxious. Searches out errors and omissions. Delivers on time.
Specialist	Single-minded, self-starting, dedicated. Provides knowledge and skills in rare supply.

Team Roles at Work (1993), R Meredith Belbin. Elsevier Butterworth Heinemann. Reproduced by kind permission of Belbin Associates: www.belbin.com.

The resource investigator will often have a great deal of enthusiasm at the beginning of a project, be a good networker and tap into contacts outside the team to gather information to bring back for an assignment.

Another two roles worth a mention are the coordinator and the shaper. Both are leadership roles, and they can be complementary roles. The coordinator observes the team, and knows the strengths and weaknesses of each person in the team, whereas the shaper will often be the one who challenges and stimulates discussion – questioning approaches, etc. Too many shapers in the team, according to Belbin, can lead to conflict, aggravation and in-fighting.

And finally, the completer. For any project it is important to have a person who is concerned about accuracy, making sure the layout of documentation is perfect, who is happy to check and recheck what is to be delivered, and ensure that the project has achieved its objective.

In reality, it is not always possible to set up an assignment or project team with exactly the right mix of individuals. If, however, you think each of the roles represents a team process, then you need to make sure that these processes all occur during the activity.

A 'no blame' approach

> The greatest mistake you can make in life is to be continually fearing you will make one.
>
> *(Elbert Hubbard, author, 1856–1915)*

If something should go wrong within your team, it is important not to automatically assume that the person who is undertaking the task is at fault. It might be that there are inhibiting factors within the organisation or team itself, poor cross-functional links, for example. It could be that your initial instructions were not as clear as they should have been, and you have not offered sufficient support during an assignment or project for that person to be able to undertake the task or responsibility appropriately.

Within your department, good news needs to be accredited to an individual in the team. The group should share bad news, and everyone should trust you as a manager to look after them in a disaster. It is important to give credit where it is deserved (you get reflected credit), and shield your staff from disasters. People clearly have to learn from their mistakes but you need to take issue with that person behind closed doors. Part of this process is to constantly be creating expectations for your people to aspire to. In continuous improvement there is no such thing as the status quo.

A recent report by the UK's Department of Trade and Industry found that many organisations claimed to have a no-blame environment until something went wrong and then everyone looked for somebody to blame! The way to ensure mediocrity is to put people at risk and then blame them for their failings; guess what, they won't expand and take risks – for fear of failing. Bill Gates claims that he will not employ a senior manager unless they have made mistakes.

> The way to ensure mediocrity is to put people at risk and then blame them for their failings; guess what, they won't expand and take risks – for fear of failing. Bill Gates claims that he will not employ a senior manager unless they have made mistakes.

The framework to monitor and measure performance

People do not like to work in a vacuum. They want to have a sense of purpose, know what they have to achieve, and where they are in relation to achieving an agreed outcome.

This means that some form of monitoring and measurement needs to be in place for the various tasks and activities that are undertaken by your team or department. You in turn as manager need to have a reliable and regular measure in place so that you can assess work flows and set objectives and targets for the future.

With a constant eye on the customer, measures should be created that are both appropriate and realistic for your team to achieve. It is a great temptation to spend much of our working lives focusing on activities, but in order to measure you need to be able to think, 'in order to do what?' So it is the results your reports need to achieve in any given period of time that is of significance.

These measures need to be not only realistic but also:

easily understood by both the members of your team and the customer;
described in detail, with a time line, and internally communicated in writing for all to see.

To create these measures, have discussions with your team from the word go to get their input, and also be flexible in approach and adapt them should you find that a particular standard is not achievable. This could be because there is a change in demand or staff ability, or because new product ranges are being introduced. In turn, it could be because you are receiving feedback from customers that the quality of service you are delivering is being impacted in a negative way. A classic example of where this can happen is in a call centre. Staff have to handle a set number of calls per hour. However, if the target does not take into account any variation in the nature of incoming enquiries and if the operative is short of time, then customers phoning in might be answered then put on hold so that the operative can achieve their target. In a nutshell, you need to keep an eye out for such anomalies and balance quantity with quality.

Let's look at this in action, and consider some of the measures that you might put in place.

Response to incoming mail
A typical standard could be response within two days, and if more time is required to source all the information requested, clarifying in the letter when a full response can be given.

Queuing system

In a retail situation, for example at the post office, how long customers might expect to be in a queue prior to being served.

Despatch

What is the procedure if a delivery is delayed? How are customers informed, by whom and when?

Sales

For an incoming potential business enquiry, the appropriate person from within your company will respond within 48 hours.

Table 3.2 shows a typical example of a council's corporate customer-care standards that would be visibly displayed in all public places within the organisation.

With any corporate standard, changes and amendments may occur over the years. Also, a department might have to modify a particular part of the standard to address their needs. For example, in the local authority standard below, if a front-line member of staff is dealing with a customer and a telephone call comes in, the manager of the department would need to have clarified in advance what should be given priority.

Monitoring and measurement will result in processes and procedures being in place. These should be regularly reviewed to ensure they have not become too cumbersome and inhibit the ability of front-line staff to serve the customer in an effective and efficient way.

To summarise, the great difference that makes a well-motivated and customer-focused team is not what they do but how they do it. It is up to you to create a culture and environment for people to flourish. Give them the opportunity to grow and develop, and learn from their mistakes. Create a clear sense of direction, giving people information in the form they can understand, and show them that you will stand by and protect them when times get tough.

Table 3.2 Example of a local authority's corporate customer care
standards

Telephones	Your call will be answered within three rings.
	You will speak to a courteous member of staff who will tell you their name and department.
	On the occasion that the person answering your call cannot help you, they will forward your query to someone who can.
	If you leave a message or voicemail, someone will get back to you within one working day.
Letters, e-mails, faxes	You will receive an acknowledgement of your query within three working days from the primary addressee.
	You will receive a reply within 10 working days.
	In the event that your query cannot be answered in the specified time, we will contact you to explain the reasons for this and give a new date for when somebody can get back to you.
Home visits	Times will always be specified and we will arrive when we say we will. If the agreed time changes, this will be explained to you beforehand.
	Staff will carry clear identification. Passwords may also be given to elderly and vulnerable customers.
Council office visits	You will be greeted by a member of staff within five minutes of arriving in one of our public reception areas.
	We aim for you to be seen within 20 minutes by somebody who is able to deal with your query. We will let you know if the wait is likely to be longer.
	Consultations will take place in a suitable and private area.

Communication	Plain English will be used in all communication with customers.
	There are services available for the visually impaired, as well as for those with hearing problems, on request.
	Translations and interpretation services will be available on request.
Complaints	We will respond to all complaints within 15 working days. On the occasion that this will not be possible, you will be provided with a new date for response.
	You can find out more about the complaints process from our website.
Staff	Staff will always be professional and respectful.
	Staff will listen to you whether you contact us by letter, e-mail or phone.
	If the initial staff member cannot help you with your query it will be forwarded, as a matter of personal responsibility, to somebody who is more able to answer your questions.
	Staff will always be identifiable by their uniforms and badges in public reception areas.
Opening hours	Any section of the council can be contacted between 9 am and 5 pm, Monday to Friday, either in person or by phone. Some offices may be open outside these hours, in which case this will be publicised.
	You can access our website at any time.
What you can do	In return we expect that you will treat all our staff with the respect and courtesy that they show you.

Key questions

- Do you 'walk the talk' – are you a visible manager or one who spends most of your time looking at spreadsheets in your office?
- Are you proactive and spread the word about the importance of your customers?
- How comprehensive is your information; do you explain and put things into context?
- Do those in your department or team have the skills and knowledge to be enabled and empowered?
- Have you created an environment where people feel challenged but happy in their working lives?

4

Effective communication with customers and colleagues

The single biggest problem with communication is the illusion that it has taken place.

(George Bernard Shaw)

Introduction

There are a variety of ways that you communicate with your team, with others within your organisation, and externally with clients and stakeholders. This can take the form of written communication, conversations on the telephone, via new media such as e-mail and video conferencing, and face-to-face contact. This chapter explores all these forms of communication plus some of the barriers that can inhibit good communication taking place.

Just think of all the different methods you can now use for communicating, or the communication methods you can use to gather information:

team meetings;
project meetings;

report writing and planning;
telephone contact, face-to-face contact;
Skype, instant messaging, WebEx;
intranet and e-mail;
real-time conferencing;
Wiki pages;
knowledge collection portals.

Collecting information to undertake a task can be comparatively straightforward; the tricky bit kicks in when you need to communicate.

As customer-care personnel we are expected to be good communicators. Good communication skills are usually a key competency when we are recruited, or when we ourselves recruit staff.

So what does 'good communication' actually mean? How does it manifest itself and why do we find sometimes that our communication gets misread or misunderstood?

The word 'communication' is derived from the Latin *communis*, meaning 'common, shared'. Until you have shared information with someone you haven't communicated it.

In addition, the person you are communicating with has to interpret the information, and there needs to be a shared understanding between both parties.

The 'shared understanding between both parties' can be trickier than you think, and there is a range of barriers that can reduce the effectiveness of communication.

Barriers to communication

These include:

Differences in perception
Our way of viewing the world will depend on our backgrounds, and people of different ages, nationalities, religions, cultures, education, status, sex and personality will perceive things differently.

Language
A range of people can talk to you differently – they could do so simply or they could use jargon or complex sentences.

Assumptions
Because of preconceived ideas we may see or hear what we were expecting to see or hear instead of what was actually done or said. Jumping to conclusions is a very common barrier.

Stereotyping
Because we learn from experiences (good and bad), there is a danger of adopting set attitudes, eg 'All teachers are the same. They think they know everything!'

Lack of knowledge
If the person trying to communicate is not really sure of themself or the receiver does not have the pertinent background information to make an informed decision, communication can be challenging.

Lack of interest
If the recipient is not interested, the communicator will have to work hard to make their message appealing.

Problems with self-expression
Some people may find it difficult to express what they really mean because of a limited vocabulary or lack of confidence.

Emotions
Emotion can be a good communication tool and also a barrier. If the emotion is too powerful it could distort the message you are trying to communicate. There may also be a hidden agenda.

Personality
A clash of personalities is a common barrier to effective communication. You may not be able to change the personality of the recipient but you should be able to control your own behaviour.

A lack of mutual trust, respect or confidence
This can have a detrimental effect on communication.

Attitude or environment
If people are in an environment that does not encourage free exchange of ideas, communication can be inhibited.

Feedback
If it is not possible to get instant feedback it is difficult to check whether or not our communication was effective.

Breaking down communication barriers

Bearing all of this in mind, the objectives of your communication should be to understand:

- **What type of person is the individual you are communicating with, in terms of personality, education, etc?**
- **How will they react to the communication?**
- **How much knowledge do they have about the topic?**
- **How much time will they have?**
- **Where will the communication take place?**
- **Will they be close enough to any relevant information or in an isolated situation?**
- **Will you be able to deal with any queries easily?**
- **When must the communication be completed?**
- **Will the recipient of your communication be too busy?**
- **Is the deadline realistic?**
- **What are the subject and purpose of the communication?**
- **What exactly needs to be said?**
- **What does the recipient need to know?**
- **What can be omitted?**
- **What information must be included so that the objectives of the communication are achieved?**

- How should the communication be effected?
- What method of communication should be used?
- How should the points be organised to ensure that a logical structure is maintained?
- How can the recipient's interest be maintained?
- How can the objectives be achieved?
- How can you ascertain that your communication has been understood? Is the method of feedback suitable?

With regard to people making assumptions, this needs a little more detailed clarification. Differentiate between fact and inference. Inferences that get turned into facts during their transmission can have serious consequences. They often cause false rumours to be spread. An inference represents only a degree of probability. It goes beyond what you are actually observing and draws conclusions that are not necessarily true, eg if you see a doctor's car parked outside your neighbour's house and you say, 'Somebody's sick over at the Smiths',' you are stating an assumption as if it were a fact. You would be more accurate if you said, 'There's a doctor's car parked in front of the Smiths' (the fact). Maybe somebody is sick there (the assumption)'.

In addition, to clarify information:

- keep the number of links in the communication chain as few as possible;
- use more than one medium for important messages;
- limit the number of items in a message;
- use illustrations and sketches to reinforce messages;
- itemise the points and put them in a logical order;
- highlight the most important points;
- use associations that will help the recipient to understand the message.

Having looked at communication barriers and what steps to take to overcome them, let's move on to the three main categories of communication:

1. putting it in writing;
2. communication on the telephone;
3. face-to-face contact.

Putting it in writing

Communicating with customers

Communicating in writing obviously has one big difference with face-to-face contact, in that you have things in black and white. This can work in two ways – to your advantage or to your detriment. The advantage is that you have proof of your thoughts and proposals. The disadvantage is that the written word is permanent and can be misread or misunderstood.

How can you make things clear and ensure that they are interpreted the way you intended?

Looking at written communication in general, how readable are your proposals, reports, internal publications, newsletters, brochures or handouts? If you think of reading a legal document – say a car-leasing agreement – how riveted are you by the copy? Do you understand it? How about the latest thriller by your favourite author? Why do you feel such a change in state when you think of these two written documents?

The answer lies in readability.

Developmental psychologists have developed the Fog Index, which gives a measure of readability based on the number of years' reading experience a person must have to understand a given type of content. Its calculations use the average number of words per sentence and the number of 'long' words (three or more syllables).

To put this into perspective, here are some comparisons:

Mr Men Books: 3–5 years
Modern action fiction: 10–12 years
The Economist: 15–20 years
Legal documents: 25+ years

So what do you need to bear in mind when creating written communication?

- **Keep sentences short, 15 to 20 words maximum. This makes the copy more readable and digestible.**
- **Be wary of the jargon you use. A series of initial such as CRM, MDU might make sense to someone within your organisation, but externally to a client they can be meaningless.**
- **Use 'spoken' writing. Think how you would express yourself if you were talking to someone, and write what you would say. Use everyday words.**
- **Avoid pomposity, trite and overused phrases – for example, 'It is my considered opinion...' 'It has come to my notice...'**

For letter writing:

- **Establish your purpose: are you writing merely to state facts, give additional information or persuade?**
- **What do you want the reader to do? Are there action points that need to be highlighted?**
- **Put yourself in the recipient's shoes. What is important to them? Use 'you' as often as possible rather than 'I'.**
- **From a layout point of view include the main points in your first (short) paragraph, go into further detail in the middle paragraph, and summarise giving clear guidelines if actions are required, and the timing involved.**

For writing memos:

- **It is important to be direct.**
- **Don't be pompous or fudge the issue.**
- **The recipient does not need to have a lengthy explanation of why you might need to cut costs or relocate equipment to a different part of the building.**
- **Get to the point in the first sentence. Don't wander around the bush and slip the key information into a final paragraph as if you are embarrassed about the situation.**

Communicating within your organisation

For routine written communication within your organisation you need to bear in mind the following:

- **More senior staff don't need to know nuts-and-bolts detail. The information you supply should be strategic and big picture: the positioning of your organisation in the marketplace, opportunities and threats.**
- **Your peers should know tactical information such as how much something will cost, what you are asking or expect from them, and how something will help your teams to work together more effectively.**
- **Team members want practical details: where they can gather information from, who will be working with whom on a project, and what budget will be allocated.**

Tailor your communication style of writing and make sure that what you are creating is what the recipient expects to receive. Sometimes you can make a mistake in what you produce if you don't ask the right questions at the time of the request for copy.

I learnt this the hard way. When I first headed up the Management Development Unit of a London university, the Dean of the Business school asked me to create a business plan for the unit. I made the cardinal mistake of not asking how comprehensive she wanted the plan to be. I produced a sizeable document of 30 or 40 pages, which took a considerable time to create. As my template, I had taken a business plan that had been passed to me by the head of the International Department, which had a substantial turnover in comparison with the business unit that I was running. It turned out that the Dean had expected a brief report of maximum 5 to 10 pages!

You need to sense the style of communication that other colleagues wish to receive, and be particularly careful when you first join a company or a new person takes over a team or a department. The written word is powerful, and you can really rock the apple cart if you decide to tackle a deep-seated problem with another business unit by writing a strident memo to the manager of that unit before you have even met them face to face.

The case study below gives the example of a breakdown in communication between two individuals in a blue-chip organisation.

It has taken the Sales Manager in this organisation several years to build a good client base, but in the last six months since the new Finance Manager has come on board, several of his key accounts have experienced problems with the Finance department. The problems have been as follows:

- Inaccurate invoicing was sent to a client's former address (even though the Sales department had informed accounts of the new address).
- One of the Sales Manager's clients had requested an invoice to be sent from his company prior to the end of their financial year so that they could pay for the services they had received within that year. One of the Account Managers in the Sales department had checked with someone in the accounts team and had been assured that this had been actioned. The Account Manager then heard from the client that he had not received the invoice in the time frame specified. She had complained to the new Finance Manager and received an inappropriately aggressive response from him, saying that he was short-staffed and no one had had the time to do it.
- The final straw for the Sales Manager was when he heard that one of his major accounts was threatening to withdraw their business from the company because of the way they had been treated by a credit control person in the Finance department. The Credit Controller had handled a late payment of an invoice

in an over-strident manner, and accused the client's Accounts department of not paying when in fact the payment had been made in the previous month.

All of these errors were small in their own right, but the end result was the possible loss of a substantial amount of revenue for the organisation.

The big mistake that the Sales Manager had made was to write a strident memo to the new Finance Manager giving few or no details of the problems that his department had experienced in the past few months. Instead the tone of the memo accused the Finance department of putting sales at risk, and accounts staff of being rude to clients.

This approach was not well received by the new Finance Manager, and a war of words continued for quite some time, all in writing, without the fundamental problems being resolved.

How could this situation have been resolved in a more satisfactory way?

Face-to-face contact should have been established between the two work colleagues when the new Finance Manager came on board. It wasn't, and strident memos between the two parties did not get their relationship off to a good start.

The Sales Manager should have presented his case in a more factual way. Staff from an analytical finance background understand data, flow charts and revenue. It therefore would have been prudent for the Sales Manager to not only present the hard facts but also the long-term financial implications of losing the named key accounts business.

Business units can often be under pressure and under-staffed, and year end in the Finance department will usually be a pressured time of year, with various business units making requests for speedy responses for their clients. Not that this is an excuse for requests to be ignored, but if the Sales Manager had established a good working rapport with the Finance department he would have had a better chance of his request being heard, actioned and given a priority.

There is always the dilemma of how much information to provide in writing in advance of a trouble-shooting meeting. Of course, facts need to be presented, but the questions are: when and how? All of the facts in this case could have been highlighted in advance, however, as no face-to-face contact had been established between the two parties. The Finance Manager could have become defensive at the meeting from the word go.

An initial 'ice-breaking' meeting could have been set up by the Sales Manager, indicating that problems had occurred between the two departments and that he would bring details to the meeting. Factual information could have then been presented face to face, with time and an opportunity then available to build a rapport between the two parties.

What can you learn from this case?

1. Face-to-face contact with key internal customers is vital, particularly when someone new joins the organisation.
2. Be careful how strident you are in memos – it can come back to bite you!
3. Understand the needs and requirements of your internal customers by building a rapport with them and asking them about the flow of work in their unit: when are their pressure times and how much lead time do they require in particular situations?

E-mail and video conferencing

E-mail has revolutionised the way we communicate with each other. It is quick, cheap, gets over the barriers created by time zones – and it can be misused.

George Bernard Shaw said that 'the more sophisticated our technology, the less we communicate'. How true this has become. In many organisations human contact seems to have been lost. All communication is by e-mail – even people sending e-mails to a person sitting next to them.

As a manager it is important for you to establish with your team the balance between using e-mail and having meetings, be they formal or informal. Establish guidelines for who should be copied into an e-mail message. So many organisations are blighted by e-mail overload, and it becomes impossible for staff to see the wood for the trees. This can often be a cunning ploy to camouflage bad news: the 100-page report sent as an attachment telling staff on page 98 that various departmental budgets are going to be cut...

A couple of guidelines with regard to creating e-mail copy:

1. Don't be tempted to use text writing; not everyone can understand it.
2. Be careful how you use humour, it can be misinterpreted by the recipient.

E-mail can be good for passing information on speedily, but it is not good for dealing with emotionally charged situations or clarifying understanding of a situation.

How about video conferencing: what are the strengths and weaknesses in using this form of communication?

The obvious strength is that you can get a group of colleagues together on different continents and they can conduct a meeting. It is a step up on telephone conference calls. A good example of this is TelePresence, developed by Cisco Systems, which creates face-to-face meeting experiences over the network, letting people interact and collaborate. In essence, you can get staff sitting around a table in a studio, and they are merged at the table with staff from other offices around the world, so the group can talk to each other as if they were sitting face to face in the same room.

Many video-conferencing facilities, however, are not as sophisticated as this. In these instances, the problem will be that you cannot look into the remote person's eyes and tell where they are looking, so you cannot tell if they are paying attention. Additionally, with some video-conferencing facilities there can be at least a one-second transmission delay, which takes away cues and makes feedback out of kilter.

Communication on the telephone

A high percentage of our day will usually be spent on the telephone, and it is obviously a practical, cost-effective way of communicating with others.

If you do not have the benefit of seeing the person you are in touch with, there are a few considerations you need to bear in mind. You can get away with a hurried or slurred manner of speaking face to face, but on the phone it can really be confusing to the recipient.

It is important, therefore, to be aware of certain aspects of voice craft when using the telephone:

Pace
Talk at a slower pace than normal. The telephone exaggerates the rate of speech. A good guide is an average of 150 words per minute. Remember that your listener could be hearing the voice of a stranger and they need time to accustom themself to you. If you speak too rapidly it is harder for the listener to understand, and misunderstanding can lead to mistrust. Similarly, if you speak too slowly the listener can become impatient and irritated.

Pitch
The pitch of your voice will vary with your state of mind. If you are excited or impatient the pitch usually rises. Because the

telephone exaggerates pitch, it is advisable to keep to deeper tones, which give you more authority.

Emphasis and inflection

Interest and understanding can be enhanced by emphasising certain words. Inflection rises if you are expressing doubt or asking a question. When the meaning of a sentence is complete, inflection drops. Most people subconsciously listen to a speaker's inflection as this often signals they are coming to the end of a sentence, so it gives them the opportunity to interject.

Face-to-face contact

Building rapport

Why is it that you can walk into a room and instantly be able to talk with ease to a particular person even if they are a stranger to you? It is because you feel you have built a rapport with that person. Building rapport is essentially a pattern-matching process where both people are on the same wavelength. Most rapport building can be without words – it is how a person projects themself through body language, facial expressions and tone of voice. If there is a mismatch between words and body language, then you instantly believe what body language is telling you.

When you meet another person, both of you will send and receive lots of 'signals' or 'messages' about the way you feel, what you think of the other person(s).

An assertive person will demonstrate positive body language, with open gestures that radiate a sense of confidence and readiness to listen to the other person.

By contrast, an aggressive person will demonstrate negative body language and will use gestures and behaviour that 'put down' the other person.

Likewise, a non-assertive person will demonstrate a different form of negative body language, which signals their feelings of low self-esteem and general lack of confidence.

When people meet us for the first time, 50 per cent of the impression they have of us comes from body language. If, for example, a person is standing quite defensively with their arms crossed, and their eyes either riveted to the ground or wandering around the room and not giving you eye contact at all, it is pretty hard to feel you can build a good rapport with that person. Going into a person's office to talk to them and finding that they don't stop what they are doing or possibly have their back to you while they pin things onto a wall chart can also be off-putting, and make you feel you want to get out of their space as soon as possible.

What can you do to make a person feel at ease in your presence? As you can see from Table 4.1, your body language should be as relaxed as possible, with arms loosely held either side of your body, and you should make eye contact with the other person.

The tone of your voice can also make a difference. If the pitch of your voice is too high it can come across as strident and off-putting. If you lower the tone of your voice and speak in a softer tone, you will create rapport with more ease.

A good technique in conversation is to match the other person's communication style. Matching is not the same as mimicking or copying. It is getting in tune with the energy level of the other person's conversation. If the person is in a hurry and wants something to happen promptly and at speed, an energetic minimal response is all that is required. If someone is unhappy and wants you to comfort them, then space and time for them to think are an important factor. We often do these things instinctively; however, there are other techniques that you can use in a conscious manner.

During a conversation, you can pick up different signals about people's preferred style. Are they visual, auditory or kinaesthetic individuals? What sort of wording might they respond to?

If an individual is a visual person, then using phrases such as 'I see,' 'clear-cut', 'beyond a shadow of a doubt' will help you communicate more effectively with them.

Table 4.1 Body language

	Assertive	**Aggressive**	**Non-assertive**
Posture	Upright/straight	Leaning forward	Shrinking
Head	Firm not rigid	Chin jutting out	Head down
Eyes	Direct no staring: good and regular eye contact	Strongly focused staring, often piercing or glaring eye contact	Glancing away, little eye contact
Face	Expression fits the words	Set/firm	Smiling even when upset
Voice	Well modulated to fit content	Loud/emphatic	Hesitant/soft trailing off at ends of words/ sentences
Arms/Head	Relaxed/moving easily	Controlled/ extreme/sharp gestures/fingers pointing, jabbing	Aimless/still
Movement/ Walking	Measured pace suitable to action	Slow and heavy or fast, deliberate, hard	Slow and hesitant or fast or jerky

Auditory individuals tune in well to expressions such as 'loud and clear', 'I hear you,' or 'Describe in detail', etc.

And how about kinaesthetic individuals – those people that are good with their hands, or maybe physically skilled, using their whole body? They will relate well to terms such as 'come to grips with', 'pull some strings' and 'Hold it!'

The importance of listening

Warren Bennis said, 'For most of us, thinking that we have "tuned in" to the other person, (we) are usually listening most intently to ourselves.'

Most people are better at talking than listening. At school or university, talking is actively promoted in the form of debate. As a student you are encouraged to take a view on a topic and vigorously defend your stance, convincing others of its worth and attacking any view that is in conflict with your stance. The problem with this form of communication is that it is very adversarial, and sets up a boxing match between competing opinions. Arguing can stop you questioning your thoughts and discovering common ground with another person.

There is a saying, 'We hear with our ears and listen with our brains.' Listening is different from hearing. It involves trying to understand what the other person is saying. When listening, you arc interested not just in the words, but in the tone of voice, what is left unsaid and the other person's body language.

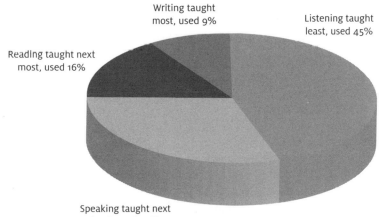

Writing taught most, used 9%

Listening taught least, used 45%

Reading taught next most, used 16%

Speaking taught next least, used 30%

Figure 4.1 Listening

Most people, however, don't listen – they just take turns to speak. We all tend to be more interested in expressing our own views and experiences than really listening to the other person's point of view. This is ironic, as we all like to be listened to and understood.

> The wise man is not the man who gives the right answers: he is the one who asks the right questions.
>
> *(Claude Levi-Strauss,* The Raw and the Cooked*)*

Listening is the most-used skill (45 per cent of our time), and in our schooling the least taught. Most people when they are not actually talking are busy rehearsing what they are going to say next.

There are five listening levels, as shown in Table 4.2.

Table 4.2 Listening levels

(Minimum listening)	1	Not hearing anything. Responding incorrectly and/or incompletely. Minimum involvement in the communication exchanges.
	2	Listening but only hearing some things. Responding incompletely. Deeper meanings are not heard. Superficial involvement.
	3	Hearing most things. Responding correctly to all that is heard. Adequate involvement in the communication exchanges. Known as passive listening.
	4	Hearing everything said and fully responding.
(Maximum listening)	5	Hearing everything said and not said, ie hearing between the lines. Responding as a result of correct interpretation of verbal and non-verbal language. Wholly involved in the communication exchanges. Known as active listening.

Why are we so often bad listeners?

First, there is the speed at which we think. The average person talks at about 125 words a minute, while the brain can think at speeds of up to 500 words a minute – so we get distracted.

Second, there are the problems of outside distractions, of tiredness, discomfort, noise, movement, phone calls, interruptions, etc.

Third, we can all interpret information in different ways. Good listening is active rather than passive. So how can you let another person know you are listening? There are a number of ways in which you can do this:

Posture
Face the other person squarely in an open posture, lean slightly towards the speaker, try to be relaxed and keep good eye contact.

Neutral responses
When listening, use non-verbal or paralinguistic signals (mm, ah) to encourage the speaker to carry on talking and to show you are listening; and watch their non-verbal signals.

Requests for clarification
If you are not clear about the meaning, ask for clarification or explanation.

Paraphrase
Restate the message in your own words, to show that you have understood correctly and to let your colleague see your interest.

Positive response
Summarise and give positive reactions before giving negative ones.

> We have two ears and one mouth so that we can listen twice as much as speak.
>
> *(Epictetus, Greek philosopher associated with the Stoics,*
> *AD 55–c135)*

A final thought to bear in mind: good listeners are not only popular, but after a while they actually know something! The fundamental capability you should have as a manager is to be an active listener, ask the right questions, stimulate thought and get others to think for themselves.

Key questions

- Are you taking into account the communication barriers there might be between you and the person you are speaking to, and adjusting your communication accordingly?
- The written word is powerful – are you using the right methodology to get across your message, and make it appropriate for the person you are addressing?
- Does your voice sound authoritative and clear on the telephone?
- Does your body language and choice of words help build rapport with others when you meet them face to face?
- Above all else, do you actively listen to gain a real understanding of what the other person wishes to communicate?

5

Breaking down inter-team and inter-departmental barriers

You cannot win if you do not play.

(Steve Forbert, songwriter, 1954–)

Introduction

Internal barriers: departments protecting their turf

'There are so many barriers between departments here, it is almost impossible to get things done!' 'You can never get help from production when you need it.' 'Our IT helpdesk takes forever to respond to a call even if you say it is urgent.' 'The legal department always has to check through contracts when we are pitching for new business. We tell them that we have to go back to the potential client with any alterations we might propose, but this has to be by a particular deadline. They don't come back to us by the deadline, so we lose the chance to go for this new business.'

These are typical of the comments that I hear when going into companies to undertake research. Departments often don't work well together. There are inter-departmental barriers that have grown up over the years, sometimes with good reason, and sometimes for no apparent reason. To give a couple of examples; those in a technical or engineering department will sometimes not work well with sales. Why is this? Possibly because the engineers and technicians are already fully stretched with maintaining the equipment on a particular customer's site. They will not have been involved at the initial stage of the sale of new equipment to this customer, and only find out once a contract has been signed between both parties that their department is going to have to support this new equipment. Needless to say, they will not always have the people in place to do this.

Another common inter-departmental barrier will be between any team or department and the Finance department. Often requests for invoices to be sent out rapidly at the end of a financial year will be sent to Finance from a whole range of different departments, with Finance simply not having the resources to cope with the extra unpredicted workload.

A breakdown in relationships between individuals, teams or departments could be as a result of the following:

- **lack of understanding of another department's workload;**
- **too much paperwork and red tape – processes and procedures that are never challenged;**
- **poor communication or interpersonal skills.**

In Chapter 3 we explored the need for processes and procedures to be regularly reviewed and upgraded if required. The way people communicate with each other is of sufficient importance to also have a chapter dedicated to it (Chapter 4).

In this chapter we are going to focus on the first bullet point above, gaining an understanding of your internal customer's workload, to make sure there is timely contact by you, in turn giving them an appreciation of your needs and requirements in order to work more collaboratively together in the future. In the second part of the chapter, we will move on to explore a variety of approaches that you can use to gain trust and influence others internally.

The internal customer

Those of us who have to deal with customers on a regular basis are all too aware that we are only as good as the back-up system we have within our organisation.

The visible one-tenth of the service you provide only works if the hidden nine-tenths operate smoothly. If you work in any part of a business and are in constant disagreement with another department, then it is not only going to be challenging to complete projects and assignments on time and within budget, but also ultimately to service the external customer in an efficient and effective way.

> The visible one-tenth of the service you provide only works if the hidden nine-tenths operates smoothly.

This is where the concept of the internal customer comes into the picture. One of the definitions of a customer is someone who requires or needs the services you provide. So think for the moment about the different teams or departments that you link with internally. These are your suppliers known as internal customers. To clarify the linkage, draw a communication map, which is similar to a spider diagram. This should relate to individuals in your company along task-related channels of communication.

This illustration will indicate your internal customers – in other words, those on whom you depend for quality, quantity, cost and time of your work. They similarly depend on you, for the lines you have drawn represent two-way communications.

To draw the map is relatively simple. Ideally it should be as comprehensive as possible. Figure 5.1 shows how it might look.

You will also need to indicate any links – the 'cross links' between the people you have shown – which do or could have a direct bearing on the fulfilment of your tasks. For example, Richard in Marketing will usually refer to Oliver in Sales before

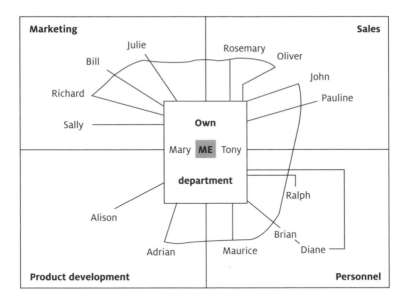

Figure 5.1 Communication map

responding to your monthly communication; similarly, John, Adrian and Maurice might have to link together before you receive the information or resources you need, and Brian appears to do nothing without first referring to Diane.

Once your map is in place you will need to indicate by some form of coding, say broken or zigzag lines, the regularity of contact, be it daily, once a week, once a month or only spasmodically. Also ideally, the means by which you mainly interact with that person (eg P = personal (face to face), E = e-mail, T = telephone). Some lines will obviously carry more than one coding.

The main purpose in drawing a communication map is to highlight where communication needs to be improved, so the next step in the process would be to indicate where communication is poor (perhaps in red), and where it is good (perhaps in green).

By going through this process you can actually isolate individuals or departments, plus the current way you communicate with them, so you can start moving forward with correcting the situation. Before beginning, it could be revealing to make a list of the ultimate repercussions that a weak link in communication can have. This will usually end up with poor service to the external customer.

Some of the reasons why your red marks are there could be: 'He dislikes receiving memos,' or 'She never bothers to pick up her phone,' or' I don't know enough about the workload or tasks they have to perform, to be able to communicate with them in the most timely or appropriate way.' Green marks could be there because 'He is on my own wavelength,' or 'We can count on each other to respond to e-mails within a day or so of a request,' or 'That person has been given the authority to make decisions on their own – they have been enabled and empowered to act'.

How should you relate to your internal customers to get the cooperation that you need to be effective?

The rights and responsibilities of colleagues

First, all parties have a right to the willing support of others in their company. However, these rights are balanced by responsibilities.

Rights: internal customers have a right to expect and receive:

1. courtesy and respect;
2. information relevant to their tasks;
3. resources necessary for the completion of their tasks;
4. freedom and opportunity to express views and opinions that contribute to decisions affecting their work;
5. understanding, if a request made of them is unreasonable or prejudicial to their personal beliefs or needs;
6. support to fulfil corporate and/or departmental objectives;
7. honest, ethical, moral and legal conduct from colleagues and those at a more senior level;
8. understanding and valuing of their contribution.

These rights come not only from basic human concerns, but also from an individual's role in the service delivery system.

In turn, there are responsibilities. These are the other side of the same coin and therefore include:

1.   being available, approachable and responsive;
2.   listening fairly and uncritically to others' views and opinions;
3.   sharing decision making when this affects others' work;
4.   providing requested information and resources;
5.   being aware of others' personal beliefs and needs and taking account of them when making requests;
6.   honouring these responsibilities by being 'other-person centred'.

Getting to know your internal customers

Let's look in a practical way at the steps you can take as a manager to get to know your internal customers and work more effectively with them.

Be proactive with information sharing. Don't hide behind your own internal departmental barrier and wait for colleagues to ask for information. Offer it to them. Offer it before they need it.

> Be proactive with information sharing.

With this in mind, if you go back to your communication map you need to prioritise which of the problem areas you wish to tackle first. This could be based on the fact that you have more contact with a particular person than with other providers, and feel that to improve your working day it would be best to explore this relationship first. Importantly, of course, your main priority should be to tackle any problem areas that are having a negative effect on the key performance indicators of the service you are providing to the external customer – the measures, targets or standards used to manage, monitor and assess the performance of your service.

Step 1

Set up a 45-minute to one-hour fact-finding meeting with
your internal customer. Of course, you need to discuss the
immediate problems you are experiencing with them, to see how
you can agree to resolve the situation. However, rather than just
focusing on negative aspects of the working relationship, you
should look to build a greater understanding between both parties
to ensure that in the future the same problems don't occur again.

Find out from them their needs and requirements when they
link with you. It might be the case that your expectations regarding
time lines and quality levels in many instances are unrealistic. Gain
an understanding of their processes and procedures, and who
within their department is responsible for each part of the workload.
There could be internal pressures with regard to their resources: for
example, in the Finance department the person who is responsible
for sending out invoices on behalf of your teams or department
might only work two days a week. So if you send through a request
for an invoice on a particular day it will not be possible for the
invoice to be sent until that person's next working day.

If an internal customer always has to supply information or
documentation to you at the last minute in a fire-fighting way,
then it could put an unnecessary strain on their resources, and
they will stop cooperating with you. Therefore, wherever you can,
plan and communicate with your supplier, and make your
requests in advance with regard to time lines and quality. You are
far more likely to get cooperation when you do have an urgent
request if you have respected the work flow of the other person or
their team or department.

Be open and find out if any of your workload causes problems
for them, and why, and discuss what can be done to remedy this.
In turn, explain your throughput of work and priorities in
particular situations, so that you can jointly agree how you should
work together in these scenarios on an ongoing basis.

In terms of supplying information to them, make sure it is as
comprehensive as possible from the word go, not fed through on a
piecemeal basis. This will give them the opportunity to schedule
time and resources accordingly.

Some organisations set up Service Level Agreements between departments, which clarify expectations between parties, but if you follow the guidelines above, you should be able to agree service provision between both parties according to the different situations that might arise.

After the meeting send the other person an e-mail thanking them for their time and summarising the key points raised during the meeting and the agreed timed action plan.

Step 2

Keeping the communication channels open is essential, so if there has been a regular problem that has occurred between both parties, then there needs to be some form of checking or feedback process in place. This could be in the form of documentation or setting up review meetings to look at progress. Feedback should focus on what is going well, and improving, as well as where there are still problem areas that need to be resolved.

> It is important to have a broader understanding of how your and your team's contribution fit into the bigger picture.

Having dealt with your request to a colleague for them to supply a service, let's move on to a colleague asking you to be a provider. The same principles apply. Explain to them your workflow and processes and the time line involved to supply the quality level of service they have asked for. There could be a degree of negotiation required here for both parties to agree what is an acceptable working arrangement between you both.

This is a good way forward as a formalised approach. However, in your role as a leader you also need to have an informal way to build understanding with your co-workers. The coffee machine is usually a good meeting point to chat to others. Find out what is currently happening in other departments or what they have planned. It is important to have a broader understanding of how your and your team's contribution fit into the bigger picture.

I was working with a group of managers from a blue-chip organisation in North-East England, and during the research phase, prior to my running training sessions with them, several of the managers voiced their concerns about the barriers between departments. So, as pre-work prior to the training, I asked a manager from each department to prepare a brief 10-minute presentation about their department. The first part of the presentation would focus on what the department actually did – their key tasks and outcomes. They were then to explain when the pressure times were in their unit and when it was best not to approach them. They were then to say when were good times to get in touch with them – this could be part of a day or a particular day of the week, etc. To add a little fun to the proceedings, I suggested that they also include any quirky, interesting facts about anyone in their group.

Each manager was to present to the rest of the attendees during the training session without interruption until they had finished. Questions and answers from the group could then follow.

It was fascinating to hear some of the comments that emerged as a result of this exercise: 'I had no idea that there were so many facets to your work.' 'Why didn't you tell us that month end, Tuesday morning, etc was not a good time to get in touch with your department?' A typical response would be: 'Well, no one ever asked.'

The interesting facts about particular people in the group brought both laughter and fascination to those that were listening. This ranged from a couple of the group undertaking the Iron Man endurance event through to one person being able to play Tibetan long trumpets (or dungchens).

This simple exchange of information proved to be a helpful first step for these managers in working with others within the organisation. Of course, this is only a first step, but the obvious idea, of finding out about the wants and needs of those you work with regularly, is common sense – but certainly not common practice.

Influencing your internal customers

In all of the cases above, the power to influence others is paramount. It could be your boss (during training programmes I usually find this is where most people want to focus!), your peers, people in other teams, or your direct reports.

What do I mean by influence? One definition says it is the process by which you persuade others to follow your advice or suggestion. I like to define it as the act or power of producing an effect without any apparent exertion of force or direct exercise of command.

Influence is:

getting what you need or want;
sustaining and enhancing the relationship.

Influence is not:

manipulation;
coercion;
command and control.

Influencing up and across your organisation

So let's start with your boss. You are the vehicle for ideas from your team to reach senior management and in turn for strategic information to be passed on to your team. The effectiveness of your team is heavily dependent on your ability to influence your manager or superiors.

When you need to put a proposition together for approval – for example, the development of a new range of services – you must be rational in your explanation of ideas and present the benefits (ie what your proposal is going to do for you or your organisation) to senior management. Your proposal or plan should be complete, not piecemeal, and, if appropriate, you should use comparative or quantitative analysis (eg figures or graphs) to win their support. You might also use surveys, actual incidents or interviews with stakeholders: in other words, those who are affected by the project and can affect it in one way or another.

If at first you don't succeed, don't give up! You need to be persistent. Ask for the support of other internal and external people to whom senior management will listen. If you can get your hands on the information, show where the same idea has worked elsewhere, and with what results. If you are successful in pushing through an idea or a particularly challenging project you will gain respect from others. Success breeds success – and you and your team will be seen as an effective work group to do business with.

> To effectively communicate, we must realise that we are all different in the way we perceive the world, and use this understanding as a guide to our communication with others.
>
> *(Anthony Robbins, US success coach)*

Building a web of influence

As a manager, your role is no longer based on knowledge and your technical abilities alone. You need to build a web of influence around you in order, for example, to be able to gain funds for projects and resources or ensure that you and your team are not perceived as the dumping ground for all the problems that others in the organisation do not wish to tackle.

What do I mean by a web of influence? People throughout your organisation, and also colleagues in other companies, can all make a contribution to working activities: sharing knowledge and informal advice. You need to invest time and effort in developing these networks.

There could be a mentoring scheme in place within your organisation. A mentor is a person at a more senior level than yourself, and usually not your line manager, who can act as a sounding board and advise you about 'political' information – for example, who the real power brokers are in the organisation. This information could be invaluable to you when you need to put a case for more funds to increase staffing levels or purchase new equipment. Even if there is not an official mentoring scheme in place, it can be well worth your while seeking out your own mentor.

Optionally, building a network of colleagues at any level in the organisation where you help each other can be beneficial. This can be as simple as calling in a favour – eg can a colleague from another team help you put together information packs for a conference as you are short-staffed on a particular day? If you find yourself in a stressful situation, for example, and you believe that undue duress has been put on you, which in your eyes has moved into bullying or harassment, it can be good to confide in a colleague for advice.

If you are calling on favours from people, there needs to be a degree of exchange, some give and take in the situation. You support them in informal ways as well – it can't be a one-way passage.

So how do you build a network of contacts? Here are a few suggestions:

Volunteer to be part of a committee.
Secondment (working elsewhere in the organisation for a temporary assignment).
Ask to visit another department or team for the day to see how they operate.
Go out with a member of the sales team for a client visit, and gain a better understanding of what they have to face.

Invite people from other teams to come into your team for the day to see the issues your group has to face.

Develop relationships with decision makers in other industry sectors, either in a comparable role to yours or at a more senior level.

The 'ambassador' role of getting both yourself and your team known throughout the organisation is vital.

> The 'ambassador' role of getting both yourself and your team known throughout the organisation is vital.

The message that precedes you

On the whole, all of us want to be successful. This is in part the simple natural desire to do well and earn the esteem of our colleagues and superiors, achieve targets and the bonus cheques that go with them. In part it is a feature of the special psychological characteristics that make customer-care staff 'people' people. Fundamentally you need to be interested in people and what motivates them. If you are not, why should they be interested in you?

Good influencing is all about inspiring people to act according to their own motivations. A successful influential manager is one who inspires a lot of people.

It follows that to obtain better results, you have to have a way of being in touch with a broad cross-section of colleagues, and doing whatever it takes to make them more likely to say yes to your ideas, requests or suggestions.

How can you do this?

Think of yourself as a customer going into a supermarket. You are faced with thousands of different kinds of foodstuffs, along with a selection of personal or household items. You are faced with two types of choice: which, of maybe up to a dozen brands, of some staple item to choose; and whether or not to buy something new.

There is no one to guide you. All you have is the label. So how do you choose? For many items you choose the same label as you bought last time you were here. But there is a first time for all of us, and our first choice is made either at random, or on price or because of a message you received before you went shopping. For foodstuffs bought in supermarkets the primary influencer is advertising.

Advertisements are often backed up by personal recommendations or warnings. Britain's consumption of cranberries a few years ago broke all records as a result of a series of recipes by a well-known TV cook and reviews in newspapers and magazines or consumer-oriented TV programmes.

Advertisements, of course, can be undermined by other information, such as press comment relating to prosecutions for poor hygiene or reports of sabotage (contaminants in Brand X) and press comment on poor personnel practices or falling market share (we like to back winners).

All of these influences work in exactly the same way in the business world. If your organisation's marketing and PR departments do a good job, people who buy your organisation's products and services will be half-convinced before they buy. If they do a poor job, they make it harder.

So how does this relate to you as a manager and your capacity to influence others?

Enlarging your web of influence

There is an invisible message that precedes you when you deal with colleagues. Do they find you good to work with or a challenge? Looking at enlarging your web of influence, the aim is to increase the number of people who 'promote' or 'sell' you to others on your behalf. They are active references who speak in a positive way about you. How many people do you work with who act as a reference for you?

> Look at enlarging your web of influence. The aim is to increase the number of people who 'promote' or 'sell' you to others on your behalf. They are active references.

Personal recommendations from satisfied managers, colleagues and clients are effective, since they involve your personal reputation as a highly competent manager.

Organisational decisions are influenced by comments from others. These may be unprompted, as when a manager happily talks about you or your team, or prompted, when others are asked questions about you. 'Nothing gets done till Peter gets involved. Nothing is too much trouble for that guy.'

Unhappy references will, of course, be only too pleased to ensure that everyone they meet knows of both their misery and who caused it.

A group of happy references prepared to recommend you and your team acts as a band of 'assistants' and clearly extends your circle of effectiveness. As your band of assistants grows, you should observe a ripple effect as your circle of effectiveness widens.

We can see this in action in the case study below, about influence in a leading accountancy firm in London.

> **Recently I was speaking to a consultant colleague of mine who worked for several years in a leading accountancy firm in London. He described how one of the partners, a VAT specialist, underestimated the importance of clarifying and promoting the services he offered to internal colleagues. The VAT partner gained all his work through the other partners. This work was thin and sporadic and his future was uncertain. My consultant colleague asked the others why they didn't involve this expert and it was because they felt he**

highlighted their mistakes, was an extra fee and clients had to pay more VAT. My colleague asked the VAT partner to think of times he had saved clients money and he wrote out 14 examples. The first was where a client owed £4 million, was being taken to court by Customs and Excise and faced a jail sentence. The partner worked on his case for a few days, got him off the court case and charges and also got him off all of the £4 million for a very nominal fee.

When this story and some of the others were sent to the partners – one each week – work began to flow in. Why had he not told the others about this? Answer: he thought it was being too pushy and like a salesman!

Help others

Active references are most likely to agree to take on 'assistant' status if you help them to achieve their own objectives. In summary, you help them to satisfy five desires:

1. to be secure;
2. to be noticed (in a favourable light) by colleagues and friends;
3. to have a sensation of well-being;
4. to possess something new (being up-to-date or a little ahead of the pack);
5. to be approachable and helpful to their colleagues.

You do this by keeping your conversations centred on the other person, since they are usually preoccupied with their own problems, motivations and desires. When you meet your internal customer colleagues, ask open-ended questions, listen carefully, explore negatives about you or your team with a view to either neutralising them or turning them to your or their advantage. Stay positive in attitude and show them esteem.

You can also increase your influence by taking every opportunity to be helpful. Your primary tool in this area is very simple: maintain the relationship. We have probably all experienced disappointment when an apparently close friend moves out of our immediate circle and then fails to keep in touch. That single missing greetings card on our birthday or at Christmas causes more pain than the pleasure we get from a fistful that arrive from people we see regularly. The lesson is clear: relationships, like motor cars, need regular servicing!

For internal customers this means dropping them a friendly e-mail occasionally, being prepared to support them if they need help in some way, and letting them know of any information that you might come across that could be pertinent to their team or department. If your colleague is in the design department, this could be flagging up information about a competitor bringing out a new product. If they are in research, it might mean new funding schemes that you hear about, and so on.

We reap what we sow

Influencers are special people. They have a particular interest in and aptitude for seeing the best in people. Liking people is as much part of their stock-in-trade as their technical skills. This gives them their optimism and positive attitude, which make it relatively easy to develop a friendly relationship with others and turn them into willing 'assistants' or active references.

Above all else, seek out like-minded people in your organisation, so that you can champion and aid each other. It can be pretty isolating trying to do everything on your own!

Key questions

- Do you understand the needs and requirements of your internal customers?
- Have you put your own case to them ?
- Have you agreed service standards between both parties and put a measuring methodology in place?
- Have you created a system of feedback to ensure continuity and development of the relationships?
- Do you put yourself in your internal customer's shoes and help them achieve their objectives?
- Have you developed a web of influence throughout your organisation in order to build your own capacity as an ambassador for your team?

Complaints, problem solving and quality improvement

There cannot be a crisis next week. My schedule is already full.

(Henry Kissinger, 1923–, German-born American academic and diplomat; quoted in the New York Times Magazine, *1969)*

Introduction

On the whole nobody notices when things go right – they expect it. However, those of us who work in customer service or customer care are only too aware that complaints occur, and in certain organisations problems are sent to us from other departments that need to be resolved. In fact, often our department has been set up to deal with these issues.

The problems could be to do with late deliveries, repairs not being done properly, customers being cross about complicated claims procedures, subcontractors not turning up on time, waiting times for a medical procedure taking too long, or promised correspondence not being sent. The list is endless, and I am sure you are only too aware of the complaints and the problems that you and your team members have to handle.

The purpose of this chapter is to acknowledge that a complaint or problem has occurred but then move on to create a positive road map for the reduction of these negative occurrences and show you how you can enhance the quality of service you offer the customer as a result of taking appropriate action. Considerable new business with a client can result from an initial complaint being handled in an effective way.

> Considerable new business with a client can result from an initial complaint being handled in an effective way.

Some complaints by customers are pretty straightforward: 'I didn't receive all the registration documents you sent. Please send the missing pages.' 'Your helpdesk person came to fix my PC but it is still not working properly.' Resolution: the missing documentation is sent again; the helpdesk person is sent out again to fix the problem. In these examples it only becomes an issue – ie a problem area that needs to be improved – if the occurrence is repeatedly identified and sourced back to the same person, who would then need monitoring or additional coaching and training.

There are other complaints and problem areas, or simply activities that need to be improved, where further analysis and attention are required, and we will look at this area in more detail in the second part of this chapter.

As a manager it is not necessarily your job to handle customers' complaints on an everyday basis. It is more likely that part of your tasks is to:

- **establish and maintain an efficient complaints-handling system (or improve an existing system);**
- **set complaint-response standards;**
- **monitor performance against those standards;**

- periodically analyse and prepare reports on complaints for senior management;
- manage, train and motivate (and recruit) the response team;
- commission (or recommend) periodic customer opinion and needs surveys;
- establish strong and continuing relationships with key customers and suppliers;
- liaise with relevant internal departments;
- manage the function overall and reflect your company's service policy in the outputs for which you are responsible;
- participate in cross-functional task groups for problem resolution.

Performance response standards

Let's start by looking at your role as a performance manager. Whatever the technology and administrative processes in your company, there are two overarching important factors that will determine the actual effectiveness of the complaint-handling system you use in your department:

1. When a customer contacts your team or department the complaint-handling system reflects the company's culture and its customer service values. A customer's experience of these will influence their perception of your company and future buying pattern.
2. Once a customer has passed through this gateway – via a complaint letter, e-mail, fax, phone call or in person – they will expect sympathetic action: a response that is attentive, understanding and quick. The majority of customers believe that right is on their side (irrespective of actual legal or moral rightness), and therefore expect to be treated as if the company or supplier is in the wrong.

However unwarranted, the very least a complainant will want is empathy – in other words, understanding that they are unhappy

with the situation, and a genuine and immediate apology from
the person responding to the call. This does not mean an
acceptance of guilt by the member of your team. They are there to
understand the customer's frustration and anger, but not more.
With this, the customer will have the chance to calm down and be
far more amenable to a negotiated resolution that is equitable to
both parties.

> The complaints-handling system reflects the company's
> culture and its customer service values.

An apology is a measure of the response standards by which
customers will judge your whole company during a complaint
situation.

Other widely established response standards include:

- **Customer care (indeed, all) staff who are not only
  sympathetic and attentive, knowledgeable and,
  importantly, enabled and empowered to act. The one
  thing guaranteed to inflame an already irate customer is
  to be passed from person to person because no one has
  the authority or knowledge to make the decision that will
  resolve the problem.**
- **Responding to an incoming call within three to five rings.**
- **Answering an incoming letter, e-mail or fax within 24
  hours. The first response can be a 'holding' one: an
  acknowledgement of the customer's correspondence plus
  a promise to write again within a specified time.**
- **Continuous updating communication (by phone, e-mail
  or letter) if the problem proves more difficult to resolve
  than first anticipated, eg a replacement item is currently
  out of stock.**
- **Openness and continuity: that is, whoever first responds
  to a customer's complaint gives their full name, if your
  company policy permits, (plus direct-line phone number**

or extension or other precise access details). If first-call resolution is not possible, make sure the agent or customer care advisor knows when to escalate a call or assign it for further investigation.

- Most customers dislike talking to an unknown person and, in the heat of the moment, can forget to ask for a name. They get annoyed having to repeat their story each time they contact the company because someone different responds. Similarly, most customers are suspicious of companies that hide behind an illegible signature purporting to be that of a Customer Services Manager; they quite rightly ask, 'As they have my name and details, why can't I have the name of a real person I can talk to in their organisation?'
- Simplicity: no one wants to achieve a resolution that in its route is more complex than the original problem. This means that documentation (purchase terms and conditions, guarantee or warranty explanations, claim forms) must be written in plain, explicit English for lay readers.
- Fairness: generally most customers want nothing more than a fair consideration of a complaint, and fair compensation; few complainants feel any need to claim excessively (and most of these will negotiate a smaller recompense if they are handled in a professional and courteous manner).

You can gain a great deal of information from complaints, and it is important to assess and analyse these issues to see how the occurrences can be diminished or completely negated.

Complaints analysis reports

These periodic reports serve a self-defining purpose: an analysis of complaints received during a preceding trading period (a week, a month, a quarter). Most analyses will list and comment on such complaint factors as:

- total number;
- number per product;
- number by type;
- complainants' genders, ages, locations and socio-economic or demographic details;
- if appropriate, the resolution of each complaint; and if not, why not;
- complaints still awaiting resolution at the time of the report;
- response performance against standards;
- costs of complaint resolutions.

Apart from complaints, where else can you identify problem areas or room for improvement?

> A pessimist sees difficulties in every opportunity; an optimist sees the opportunity in every difficulty.
>
> *(Winston Churchill)*

Resolving problems; quality-improvement activities

Problems, like change, are normal. You and your team need to be perceived as problem solvers, not problem receivers. The trick is to ensure that reacting to problems does not overtake you. Finding solutions involves thoughtful planning and sensitive implementation and, above all, consultation with, and involvement of, the people affected by the problem.

What many managers miss is that when they go about solving problems they don't get to the root cause; they only treat symptoms. To reach a successful outcome, it is vital to get to the underlying reason why problems have occurred.

How should you take things forward? As depicted in Figure 6.1, there are four stages that you need to go through during any problem-solving or quality-improvement activity:

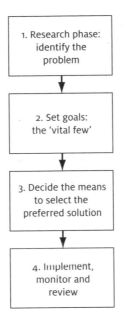

Figure 6.1 Problem-solving flow chart

Stage 1. Research phase: identify the problem.
Stage 2. Set goals: the 'vital few'.
Stage 3. Decide the means to select the preferred solution.
Stage 4. Implement, monitor and review.

Let's examine each of these stages in more detail.

Research phase: identify the problem

This first phase of activity involves researching all your existing sources of information to identify potential problems to be resolved.

We have already mentioned complaints as a good starting point for identifying what needs to be improved. Other sources where you can gather information include:

- **customer surveys or market research reports;**

- **customer needs assessments;**
- **product user groups;**
- **meetings with customers;**
- **using the six satisfaction elements model.**

We looked at customer surveys and research in Chapter 2. There is a detailed description of the six satisfaction elements model in Chapter 1, but it could be useful to see how a particular organisation, a private hospital, used this model to identify problem areas and where they believed quality needed to be improved.

As a reminder, the satisfaction elements are:

1. the product or service;
2. sales;
3. after-sales;
4. location;
5. time;
6. culture.

The top team and department heads got together for a half-day session, to analyse what was of real importance to the hospital's customers (patients, specialists and consultants who used the hospital facilities). The group of 20 was divided into four.

When they went through the different elements systematically they came to the conclusion that the in-patient experience was excellent. However, the hospital's car park was poorly lit and this led to complaints both from patients and staff due to feelings of insecurity, especially at night. A couple of the groups also felt that the snack-food trolley was only available for a limited part of the day, and they had received verbal feedback from patients complaining about this. Even though the person responsible for marketing was present, several of the groups commented on the inadequacy of documentation – brochures and so on – and the general view was that the website needed to be updated and enhanced.

This short exercise was a useful way of broadening out the approach for collection of information that was pertinent to customers' experience. The information would probably not have been captured with other research methods, as it often came down to the subjective views of particular individuals who would not normally be completing customer care questionnaires.

As we have mentioned in Chapter 1, customers are assessing the service in a breadth of ways (the satisfaction elements). In this instance, the patient coming to the hospital for a procedure could have been very happy with the operation they had received, but lack of security in the car park and no way of getting snacks in the evening could have damaged their overall perception of the quality of service they received from the hospital.

Set goals: the 'vital few'

Once you have identified the problem areas to solve and improvements you wish to make, you must identify the vital few goals to take forward.

The concept of the vital few is based on the 80/20 principle, also known as the Pareto principle after an Italian, Vilfredo Pareto, who established that 80 per cent of the wealth of a nation is invariably owned by 20 per cent of its population. Transferring this to the business world, you will probably find that most of your issues will come from a small number of causes. You could also observe that most of your complaints come from a small number of customers, not the majority. And also that 20 per cent of your effort produces 80 per cent of the results.

> Identify the 'vital few', using the 80/20 principle.

Having identified specific problems and the quality improvements required, you must set goals before you take action. The purpose of goals is to keep you on track, motivated and focused on the actions you need to take. As shown in Table 6.1, these goals need to be concrete (what exactly and by when), and also have SMART goals – or, sometimes – SMARTER goals. So what do we mean by this?

Table 6.1 SMART(ER) goals

Term	Explanation
Specific	giving a clear description of what needs to be resolved
Measurable	in terms of quality, quantity and cost
Achievable	includes gaining the agreement of your manager and your team
Relevant	specifying the business need to be satisfied
Time-bound	in terms of completion date and monitoring
Ethical	alternative term: exciting
Reviewed	alternative term: rewarded

Let's look at the use of SMART in action. Below you will see a communication from a manager to his team, which left them confused and not really understanding the message. What are the problems with the communication and why do you think team members might find it difficult to understand? In the second box you will find the answers.

> **Management has decided to outsource all the organisation's service activities, such as mail rooms, training, transportation, etc to reduce costs by 7 per cent this financial year.**
>
> **The reason for this is a move to a concentration on core activities only so that the organisation can manage its operations more effectively and satisfy shareholders by increasing profitability and overall cost effectiveness by 5 per cent.**

> The benefits will be more specific delivery and service targets from these suppliers and allow all personnel to concentrate on delivering their objectives.

Why was this communication not SMART? Here are the reasons why.

> Management has decided to outsource all (what does 'all' mean? Is there a list?) the organisation's service activities, such as mail rooms, training, transportation, etc to reduce costs by 7 per cent this financial year. (When does management expect these changes to start?)
>
> The reason for this is a move to a concentration on core activities (what core activities?) only so that the organisation can manage its operations more effectively and satisfy shareholders (what does 'effectively' and 'satisfy shareholders' mean?) by increasing profitability and overall cost effectiveness by 5 per cent. (Does management expect manpower to be impacted? Can we impact it?)
>
> The benefits will be more specific delivery and service targets (what are these, exactly?) from these suppliers and allow all personnel to concentrate on delivering their objectives. (How will objectives change?)

So let's look at SMART in action by returning to the hospital example. The Manager of the Booking department had a variety of responsibilities. In a brainstorming session with his team, areas were clarified that they wanted to improve, and they used SMART objectives to take things forward. They identified a number of areas for improvement. Table 6.2 shows three examples.

Table 6.2 Hospital example of SMART objectives

Patient goal	Objective	Lead person	Due date	Evidence	Three-month progress review
Ensure we deliver the best care standard with resources available	Ensure there are no more than three justified, written complaints about the booking department in one year	P Taylor	4/2009	Number of written complaints	

Consultant and general practitioner goal	Objectives	Lead person	Due date	Evidence	Three-month progress review
Ensure we deliver the highest-possible standard of service to consultants and general practitioners	1. Compile a directory of 'length of time' for standard operations, noting variations between consultants to assist in judging admission times and duration of theatre slots 2. Create a directory of consultant signatures to ease identification of out-patients' booking documentation	P Taylor with C Hogarth	6/2009	Directory	

Building and equipment goal	Objectives	Lead person	Due date	Evidence	Three-month progress review
Maintain facilities to the highest standards to ensure health and safety	1. Redecorate waiting rooms and reception areas 2. Fix faulty drainpipes and guttering	C Jones	5/2009	Repairs and decorations completed	

Since the Booking department was part of a hospital they used the term 'evidence' for monitoring the outcome. You could use the term 'objectives achieved' in your version.

Decide the means to select the preferred solution

So you have clarified what the problem is or the quality improvement to be made. Now you need to consider which approach you want to adopt to define or analyse the situation to take things forward by using practical problem-solving techniques.

Practical problem-solving techniques

Get your team together and start by flushing out a range of ideas and approaches to move things forward, selecting from the following techniques.

Brainstorming

Have someone list all the ideas from the group as quickly as possible, without any evaluation of ideas. Gather as many ideas as you can as quickly as you can. This list can then be shortened and a final solution developed from the best items.

Brainwriting

Each person records an idea or solution to the problem on a piece of paper and adds it to a pile. Everyone then takes a different paper from the pile and adds an idea related to the one already on that page. They write down the first thing that comes to mind. These ideas can then be compiled and discussed to develop a final solution. This is often successful in a quieter group, when it is difficult to get everyone talking.

Dotmocracy

Having undertaken brainstorming or brainwriting, provide each person with the same number of dot stickers or pennies or tokens. Vote individually on the list of brainstormed alternatives.

If someone feels strongly about one item they are welcome to put all their dots on that item. The alternative with the greatest number of dots is the decision preference.

Nominal group technique

Each person shares their ideas. Someone lists all the different ideas. Everyone then ranks their preferences individually from the whole list, scoring them from 1 to 10. These scores are added together and a group score is given. This gives priorities on a group basis. Note that if the number 1 is used to rate an individual best choice, then the list item with the smallest group score is the most desired.

Criteria matrix

Develop a set of standards on which each alternative is judged. Some examples are:

- **costs;**
- **risks involved;**
- **timeliness;**
- **convenience or satisfaction.**

The matrix looks like a table, with the alternatives down the left side and the criteria across the top. Each alternative is ranked by the criteria you have opted to use (1 to 5, yes or no, etc) and the scores are added up at the bottom.

When you need to get down to the 'vital few', try these techniques.

Bubble-up/bubble-down

This is used for ranking statements or ideas, or putting ideas in an orderly sequence. Read the first two statements, decide between the two which statement is least preferred and should be eliminated. Now compare the statement left to the next one on the list and continue to do this until you have reached the last item on your list and the group is satisfied. For example: when you are buying a house, it is much easier to compare the house you're viewing with the last house you viewed. After evaluating how this one rates, you eliminate one of the two. The preference between the two is the only house used in future comparisons.

Lateral thinking

Getting both yourself and the team to 'think out of the box' is important. Lateral thinking is a way of solving problems by apparently illogical methods. It involves an element of provocation to jerk our minds out of the usual pattern.

The management guru Dr Edward de Bono defines lateral thinking in illustrative form as: you cannot dig a hole in a different place by digging the same hole deeper. This is like politicians saying there is no point doing the same thing over and over and expecting a different result. Trying harder at the same things or putting more effort into doing them may not be as useful as changing direction. De Bono suggests dividing a problem into parts so that one part does not create a monopoly of attention. The objective in using this approach is to shift your thinking from a negative to a positive stance; from thinking emotional reactions to facts. You can read more about this in *Six Thinking Hats* by Edward de Bono (LittleBrown and Company, 1985).

This is my take on de Bono's approach:

Step 1. Gather all your facts and figures together, and make sure you have all the information you require.
Step 2. Have a clear idea of what you want to have happen in x time frame (this could be a week, a month or years). In other words, you need to have a strategy and forecast the future and what it is going to look like.
Step 3. Consider all the information you have to hand with caution, and question what might be wrong with it. For example, is the brief completely clear or are there ambiguities?
Step 4. Think in a positive way – look for the good in the situation. The 'glass half full' approach rather than 'glass half empty'!
Step 5. Use 'emotional intelligence'. What do you individually and jointly feel about this? Does it excite you, or make you feel uncomfortable?

Step 6. Build on your original ideas. Be creative. What will add value?
Step 7. Pull everything together and develop a plan with a time
line. Organise the details: who will do what by when, and how will
things be monitored?

During lateral-thinking sessions, teams often get bogged down at
the data-and-information stage and keep asking themselves 'What
information is missing?' Or they focus on Step 3, the cautionary
stage: 'It will never work,' 'Senior management won't accept our
recommendations,' etc. They forget to direct their thinking as to
how they can approach things differently, be creative or use their
intuition and simply follow a hunch.

Using the method above facilitates the free flowing of
information. Creativity does not come from special types of
people. Creative thinking can apply to everyone. Different
methodologies help by getting people to look at situations in
different ways and push through creative dry spots.

So much of this comes down to time. We are all task driven,
often with tight deadlines to achieve. You need to allocate time for
broader thinking and getting together on a regular basis to review
quality and discuss how to reduce complaints and stop them
escalating into major problems that need to be resolved.

Implement, monitor and review

So you have put in place what you plan to do with regard to a
problem resolution or quality improvement. It's important to have
commitment to the final plans from everyone before any action is
put into motion.

Monitor the results of your decisions and the impact on others
regularly. You may need to make minor changes as you go.

What are practical questions to ask during the monitoring and
review stage?

Always ask your questions positively. Never threaten or
blame if mistakes are made, or the project is not on track. What's
done is done. You need those in your team who have made the

error to realise for the future how to make sure it does not happen again.

Ultimately as the manager you have responsibility to ensure mistakes do not recur and that problems are solved quickly and decisively. How can this be done? By constantly asking questions to find solutions and capture learning. A five-minute chat can make all the difference.

Ask:

What's going well or what did you set out to achieve?
What actually happened?
Why did that happen?
What should we do differently next time?
What action should we take?

> Experience is the name everyone gives to their mistakes.
>
> *(Oscar Wilde,* Lady Windermere's Fan, *1892)*

You should also consider the need to monitor your environment. It is important to know if there is any risk that could scupper or stall your plans. Ongoing communication with all those involved (the stakeholders) is vital, plus with the leaders of any projects you are depending on.

There are, needless to say, risks involved that can prevent your problem-solving project from succeeding. These could be changing priorities, inadequate resources (people, money, time), lack of senior-management sponsorship, staff turnover, key players unable or unwilling to participate, other projects not getting completed on time, economic change, etc. Of course, the list will be different in each instance, and the probability that any particular risk will occur varies as well. The key is to identify them and assess each one for probability of occurrence and impact on the plan if it should occur.

You need to develop contingency arrangements immediately for anything that has both a high probability of occurring and a high impact. You may also want to develop contingency plans for low-probability/high-impact issues. Low-impact issues, especially if the probability is low, are probably not worth significant contingency planning.

Key questions

- Do you have robust response standards for complaints, which leave the customer thinking 'This is a good organisation to be dealing with'?
- You are not a one-person show. Do you use a variety of methodologies to stimulate ideas from your team?
- During problem-solving and quality-improvement activities:
  - Do you and your team select the 'vital few' and use SMART goals to achieve your objectives?
  - Do you use a structured approach to move forward?
  - Do you assess what might happen if things don't go to plan? Have you got a contingency plan in place?
  - Do you monitor and review once the initial problem-solving or quality-improvement activity has happened?

Building long-term customer relationships

> It's getting clearer every day that becoming obsessed with customers is the only survival route in today's crazy environment.
>
> *(Tom Peters,* Thriving on Chaos*)*

Introduction

Too many organisations make a sale and walk. They walk away without giving a second thought about how to continually engage with these 'one-time' customers. As a manager responsible for customer care you might not directly have the power to implement incentive or loyalty schemes that are set up either by the Sales department or corporately. But you certainly need to be aware of how they operate and of the pros and cons of using this method of promotion to sustain a loyal customer base. In turn, as you will see in this chapter, there is much that you and your team can do to ensure that customers remain loyal to your organisation.

Let's face it, the simple fact is it is easier and less expensive to retain existing customers and keep key customers than to attract new ones. It is generally agreed that loyal customers tend to spend more than promiscuous ones whose loyalty has to be constantly re-won.

Why is this? It's all about the way your organisation positions itself. You are what you are in the minds of your customers. Or, to put it another way from the customer's perspective...

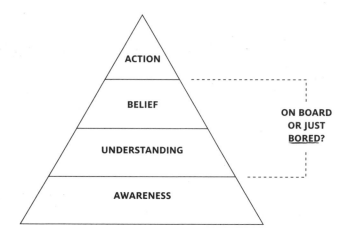

Figure 7.1 On board or just bored?

But of course you have to attract customers in the first place, and one of the devices used is some form of discount or incentive scheme.

Incentives and loyalty schemes

An incentive scheme – 'Buy one, get one free,' 'Have your car washed here three times and the fourth time is free' – can seem genuinely enticing. But the 'Fly to Berlin for £5 plus taxes' can seem less enticing and frankly rather annoying to a customer when they go on to the airline website and find that additional taxes and surcharges wreck the low-price promise.

Satellite and cable television or telecoms organisations love to talk about increasing retention rates but then recruit new customers via price promotions and free sampling – techniques that draw out of the woodwork precisely those customers hardest to keep. The problem is that these recruitment efforts could merely load the pipeline with people who are inherently disloyal. Of course, suppliers cannot afford not to keep finding new customers, and such fairly non-arbitrary promotion tools play a useful role in raising awareness, interest and motivation in potential purchasers.

> Don't attract the 'wrong' customers.

Suppliers know they will experience some customer loss once the promotion period ends. Their hope is that enough customers will stay not only to cover the costs of the promotion and of administering customer acquisition and pipeline loss – but also to grow their base of retained customers who by definition are likely to be the long-term loyal customers whom they need. This is a self-pruning process that sorts out the promiscuous from the stable.

Blanket customer marketing doesn't work. It's inherently wasteful since this approach draws off resources that should be used to retain and, importantly, reward just those customers who are actually or highly likely to be loyal customers even without the magnet of the special offer. Their magnet will be the six satisfaction elements and confidence that their individual needs will be met. These customers will have been identified and measured by their retention rate and their estimated lifetime value.

Satisfied customers feel good only as long as their current needs are met and only as long as they perceive that a supplier is giving value. Committed customers want more than transient bait. They want to develop a long-term relationship with an organisation that understands and responds to their individual needs, and discriminates between customers who have been genuinely loyal over a period and newcomers who have yet to demonstrate such an allegiance.

This raises the question of whether customer care schemes are designed to reward true loyalty or to lure customers indiscriminately with an incentive.

With this in mind, how about loyalty schemes such as pharmacy-style 'advantage' cards, supermarket club cards, and airline rewards cards? A loyalty scheme can be a highly valuable addition to a customer-care initiative. However, setting up a scheme can have pros and cons.

Table 7.1 The pros and cons of loyalty schemes

Pros	Cons
An incentive to the customer to purchase from you	Are they the target customers you should be attracting?
Chance to build long-term relationships	Set-up costs
Marketing opportunities	On-costs that must be covered by attracting increased sales
Competitive edge	Reward(s) that might not be sufficiently motivating to win long-term loyalty
Increased sales	Redemption processes that might be too complex for customers
Customer research data	The time and money it would take an average customer to accumulate sufficient points for a worthwhile reward
Foundation for tie-ins to additional offers	Loyalty can be to the incentive rather than the supplier, which could mean loss of business once the programme ceases

Despite the potential downsides of establishing a loyalty scheme, many schemes are immensely successful. In the UK, for example, many shoppers know exactly the benefits and differences between Tesco's and Sainsbury's club card schemes. That's quite a result!

While a loyalty scheme is not a substitute for such core values as product quality and customer service, it can attract customers who might be willing to test how well their needs are met. Air Miles schemes have been shown to retain customers' loyalty due to the benefits of free flights available to family and friends, and many of the airlines' schemes move regular purchasers into different reward brackets as they increase spend.

Of course, it is not only retail companies that can benefit from offering a loyalty scheme. Commercial and industrial suppliers, however, seem not to pay sufficient attention to developing loyalty among their key purchasers.

As a customer care manager, how can you find out what is important to your key customers? My definition of key customers is those who purchase from you on a regular basis and through analysis have been proven to be profitable customers. The answer, of course, is to ask them!

This could be done as a research project or by one-to-one interviews, depending on the number of key customers that you might have. You could do a SWOT analysis to find out the strengths and weaknesses of what you offer the marketplace, be it a product or service. During the analysis process you could also explore the strengths and weaknesses in the service level of your department, where you can take immediate action.

Ask the department:

Strengths

What do we as a company do well with regard to the products or services we offer the marketplace? How about our department – what do we do well?

Weaknesses

Where is there room for improvement? Once again, start at corporate level and then focus on our own department.

Opportunities

Could you suggest any other companies that might be interested in our products or services? With regard to the service that our department offers, are there any recommendations that you can make to improve the standard of care we offer them?

Threats

Are there any changes that might be occurring in our customers' environment that might have an impact on the budget they are currently spending with our company? Are there any new competitors for us to be aware of that might impact on our business?

You will be able to gather information that specifically relates to your department and take appropriate action according to the findings that emerge. There will also be information that you will need to share corporately within your organisation, so make sure that this information is documented and taken to a more senior level. This could result in the forming of a cross-functional team (for example, customer service, product development, distribution and finance) to take things forward.

Incentives are just one of the factors from just one of the six satisfaction elements. They alone will not guarantee loyalty, particularly if a competitor offers a bigger and better incentive and if it is a prime purchase motivator. An incentive scheme can be a powerful attractor, but can you put your hand on your heart and say, 'People came to us originally for the price offered during a promotion but stayed because of the service'?

How to develop an ongoing business relationship with customers

Corporate loyalty schemes have their place, but what can you personally do to develop rapport with the customer and encourage them to continue doing business with your organisation? Sales personnel and the Business Development department will have immediate and ongoing relationships with clients. However, a Customer Services department will engage with regular purchasers or customers on a service contract that the department is responsible for implementing, or it may simply deal with customers making a complaint. So you as a Customer Care Manager can still play your part in enhancing the profile of the company and also flag new business opportunities to pass through to the business development team.

A manager's roles in customer care can be very diverse. In one environment you could have literally hundreds of customers that your team or department service. In other circumstances you could be looking after two or three main customers who have been passed to you for after-sales service activity. Regardless of whether it is two or two hundred customers that you deal with, there are always going to be occasions when you want to develop or build the relationship with particular customers. So how do you do this, without appearing to be a pushy sales person?

Building relationships during a service contract

If your team is responsible for carrying out any type of service contract where continuous customer contact is required, for example the installation of a product or service, then I am sure you already have built into your project schedule regular review meetings with the customer, asking variations of the following questions:

How are our recommendations working?
Speaking now from experience, how does our solution to your business problem measure up?
Is there anything else we can do or arrange to improve your experience of our product or service?
Are there any other issues that have arisen since we last met that you would like to discuss, where we might be able to help?

And, of course, you thank them if they have recommended your organisation or your department to any new potential customers.

Build a 'trusted advisor' relationship with your customers.

The main point in any of these discussions, as has been clarified in depth in the chapter on communication, is to keep the conversation customer-centred. Keep focusing on what's important to them. They do the talking, you do the prompting and steering of the conversation. Your main aim is to build a 'trusted advisor' relationship with your customer by showing genuine interest, not just in the immediate topic you are discussing, but also in broader picture issues. For example, they don't work in isolation, so there could be considerations in how they achieve outcomes that are impacted by internal issues within their company. See Figure 7.2.

In this service capacity, you will often identify opportunities for new business. Make sure you pass all these leads through to your company's sales team to follow up. This might seem glaringly

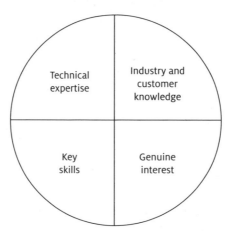

Figure 7.2 The genuine interest circle

obvious, but you would be surprised how often during research assignments on a client's site, both I and other consultant colleagues have seen new business opportunities that are missed by non-sales staff. For example, the delivery person who finds out that the customer would like more information about a particular new product your company are promoting and does not pass this lead through to the sales team; or the service engineer who sees that your department needs to upgrade its PCs but doesn't let their sales team know about this; and so it goes on.

Building customer relationships for all managers in customer care

For any manager in customer care there will always be customers who need to be nurtured in a special way. They could be key account customers or those who have made a significant complaint and who need to be treated with kid gloves to ensure they don't take their business elsewhere.

Over a period of time while dealing with a customer, you should get to know quite a lot about them as an individual and their particular interests both in and out of the workplace. So send them clippings from magazines and newspapers and any other oddments that come your way and might interest them. Put Google Alerts into your search engine and you will receive e-mail updates on the organisations you select. Google Alerts is a very handy way to receive the latest relevant Google web news results based on your choice of query or topic. You can use it to monitor customers, competitors or any sector of your choice.

You could have ideas about how the customer can extend their areas of influence. Perhaps on a trip abroad you spot a market or some other opportunity they could exploit; you may come across information about their competitors which could be of interest to them.

Free samples of a product always go down well, and if you are developing new ideas for a service that you are responsible for, include them in a customer panel during the creation stage. If, for example, you give them a book that has been written by you or by a colleague from your company, stick your business card on the inside cover. Should they attend one of your training sessions or a seminar that you organise, if you or the trainer used PowerPoint for the presentation they will have probably been supplied hard copy during the session. The day after the event e-mail an electronic copy to your special customers and follow this up later with a phone call.

You will ensure that your key customers are always invited to appropriate company-sponsored social occasions: the Christmas drinks party, the golf day, as well as your pavilion at trade fairs or at sporting or cultural events. You will make sure that they are on the mailing list for company customer magazines and Christmas cards. For any regular mailshots you send out from your department, try to add a handwritten personal comment on the documentation to show that you are taking care of them personally.

All these are small reminders that they are important to you and that you care. This means you have more of a chance that your client will respond in kind and automatically continue to do business with you.

Great, you have built a good working relationship with your customer. What then? Answer: build on this goodwill to create more business.

Referrals; the active reference principle

Be proactive and ask your customer if they will be an 'active reference'. You could go about this by saying, 'We have worked together for a time now; are you able to introduce me to any other contacts in your organisation, or elsewhere, that we might talk to?'

You might get a no – but there is a good chance that you will get a yes if they are happy with the product or service you offer and can see that their colleagues could benefit from working with you. The point here is that if you don't ask, you don't get!

It should be a win–win situation for both parties. If they believe in you and your company's offerings, they will get reflected glory by recommending you to others (obviously subject to them also being happy with what you have to offer).

Active references are different from passive references. When the customer agrees to be a reference for you, they will talk to others on your behalf. If you just use their name to get into other parts of the organisation, without checking with them first, this is a passive reference. What is the advantage of an active reference? If your organisation makes a mistake and your customer is your active reference, they are more likely to defend you. Passive references generally will never do that.

Effectiveness of corporate activities in building long-term customer-care relationships

Going back to where we started in Chapter 1, you will see that there is a plethora of activities that organisations do to attract business to their organisation. As time progresses, how useful are these activities in building a long-term relationship with a customer?

Detailed in Table 7.2 are three blocks of activities. You will see as time progresses which activities are the most productive and effective.

You will see that all the activities that are undertaken initially to attract business – such as advertising, non-selective ballroom-style seminars, cold calls by the sales team – ultimately fade into the woodwork and are less effective as the business relationship develops with the customer.

To round off this chapter; no organisation can rely solely on loyalty schemes and incentives to 'buy' customer loyalty. There needs to be more, and this all comes down, as I have said repeatedly throughout this book, to people. You and your team are not only there to service customers but also to build their loyalty.

Table 7.2 Activities to build longer-term relationships with customers

Most effective	Research the customer's business
	One-to-one relationship building
	Seminars (small scale)
	Articles in customer-orientated (sector) press
	Speeches at customer industry meetings
Less effective	Community or civic activities
	Networking with potential referral sources
	Newsletters
Least effective	Public relations
	Brochures
	Seminars (ballroom scale)
	Direct mail
	Cold calls
	Sponsorship of cultural or sporting events
	Advertising
	Video brochures

Key questions

- **How do you look after your key customers – do they get special treatment?**
- **Are you being proactive in seeking ways to develop the relationship of these customers?**
- **Apart from operational activities, do you expand your role to include subtle ways of enhancing the profile of your company and the development of business?**
- **Do you get your customers to act as active references?**